Crossroads

By
Winifred Jeanette Franklin

Copyright © Winifred Franklin 2018
All rights reserved

Edited by
Adinas Henry

Acknowledgements

I would to thank all of these wonderful people:

Theresa Kay, Robin Kay, Adinas Henry, Venessa Franklin, Melanie Jenkins, Courtney Henry, Florence. Victoria Reynolds (deceased) Bill Reynolds (deceased) Ted Reynolds and George Reynolds. We thank you all for the loving and happy memories and also to everyone else who helped shape and form this book.

Introduction

'Crossroads' is an up close and personal true story of Winifred's life. It takes you through her amazing experiences of growing up in England; with various accounts of her life in early childhood and her youthful romance. Winifred, tells of the hardships endured by the many struggling families during the depression years and World War 2. The subsequent effects had a substantial impact, not only on her life, but on the people all around her. This book is set to become a 20th Century sensation, for not only is it a literary gem, it also is of great historical value, for the scholar and for those interested in what life was like living in Britain during the 1930's and 1940's. It would certainly make for a great mini-series for its depiction of the various characters created from that era.

Winifred starts her story off in the first person, to create a personable feel for the reader; she then changed her story to the third person as it reads like fiction with all the colorful characters evolving. The reader must remember that everything in this story is actual facts of what happened in Winifred's life; hence the story is a historical document as well. It is delightful to read, heartfelt, funny and also at times will have you in tears so be ready with your tissue boxes.

Chapter I

The light and the dark shadows danced in grotesque shapes on the freshly painted green and cream walls, at times, reaching out, in mythical movements, towards the well baked off-white of the ceiling. A loud ticking alarm clock, from its place of importance on the mantlepiece, disturbed the silence of the room, acting like a hypnotist's metronome on the man sleeping in the deep old fashioned arm chair. Singed hair tumbled boyishly about his once handsome face. The slightest movement he made brought sounds of moaning from swollen lips. Flashing firelight revealed the cause of the pain. Blisters that hung in bunches' like grapes, almost the size of walnuts, decorated his shoulder and wove themselves right down one side of his body.

I slowly opened the door so as not to disturb my father and tiptoed my way across towards the wreckage of human flesh slumped in the chair. I was a child of seven with large curls of hair that ran down to my shoulders now sparkling gold in the bright glow of the flickering firelight. I had large blue eyes that held the fathoms of the ages in them; such was the wisdom bestowed upon me. Looking at my father's exposed burnt raw flesh, tears welling up in my eyes, bending down I planted a kiss on his forehead. Picking up my rag doll from the chair that cradled him, I left the room.

Halfway along the narrow hallway a loud knocking on the door startled me. "Mommy, is that you?" I yelled.

"Yes, dear, hurry and let me in."

Balancing on the tips of my toes, I reached up to the door knob and turned it. A woman entered carrying a small frail child. She went into the kitchen and laid him down on the old couch tucking a blanket around him. On entering the hall again, I called out to my elder sister Milly - she appeared, sleepy-eyed from the back bedroom, looking older than her nine years. Her long almost snow white hair had been cut very short. Our cousins from next door had played at curling it round sticks of wood soaked in kerosene bought for a farthing a bundle at the local shop. The splinters from the wood had tangled her hair beyond hope of repair. Her hair had been cropped close to the scalp, giving somewhat of a boyish look to her appearance. All the same, she did not lack charm and a good measure of humor, her witticisms being a byword among her family and friends. When she went to school the white badge she wore showed her to be the top of her class. Now she busied herself laying cups and saucers on the large wooden table, making as little noise as possible for fear of waking her father.

Milly gently shook her father. He coughed and moaned and finally woke up. Automatically he glanced at the clock, "You've woken me ten minutes late Milly. Where's your mother?"

"She is sleeping."

"What did the doctor say about him?" He asked nodding painfully in the direction of the sleeping child.

"Mum never said." replied Milly

Turning towards the table Milly gathered up clean strips of flannelette and began to gently bandage his burnt arm, looking as she finished, for the praise which was sure to follow.

"Top job nurse, now get me tea batches, while I do me leg."

Eagerly she fetched them for him. This consisted of condensed milk, sugar and tea all mixed together, enough to make several pots of tea. It was then placed in grease proof paper and twisted into a bundle just large enough to fit into a side pocket together with the sandwiches so preventing him from leaving his lunch behind on the tram, for at times he found it difficult to stay awake.

Milly stood on a chair in order to help him on with his overcoat which hung heavily on the blistered parts of his body. Assisting her down, he bayed her good night. A worried expression crossed his face as he looked down at his sleeping son. He stepped out into the cold night and was soon engulfed by darkness.

A tram came zigzagging along the lines situated along the middle of the roads. A few passengers waiting to board behind him became impatient at his apparent slowness, "What's the matter mate, not awake yet? Get a move on will yer." This was followed by much pushing. They all seemed determined to get in out of the cold, even for only a short time. Jack then became aware of a trickling sensation as fluid began to ooze from his blisters and run down his body. They had been broken up by the pushing. He let out such a cry of anger and pain that they all fell back from him. This brought the conductors down from collecting the tickets upstairs.

"Steady on all of yer. Steady on, ere let's get this bloke up from the floor shall we. What's the matter mate, had one too many?" He bent over Bill, but seeing the state of his face, exclaimed, "Core blimey mate, fell in a fire did yer? Yer shouldn't be out on a night like this." He helped him onto a seat close to the entrance so he could keep an eye on him.

"Core, the size of them blisters, funny how only one side of his face is burnt." The other passengers, now seated, constantly peered back at him. He was unaware of this for fresh pain had brought waves of blackness before his eyes, which he desperately strove to fight off. By the time the tram came clanging to his stop he had recovered enough to alight without help, or so he thought, for people sitting next to him had other ideas and treating him, in his eyes, like a docile old man. They proceeded to grab him by his arms thinking to help him down the tram stairway into the street.

As he walked away, he waved his good arm, shouting imprecations of a dire nature causing the conductor in consternation to exclaim, "I dunno, there's something funny about 'im besides his face, there's no pleasing some people."

Wiping off beads of perspiration from his face Bill began his walk to the gasworks. The huge cylinders could be seen from miles away, great rounds of steel that held men in their grip. They stank of the gas they slaved to make – even their food tasted of it. It was often said that they would lay their uncooked food in pans on the floor and it would cook in the intense heat given out by the furnaces.

Opening the side door of the retort house, one would witness a sight not far removed from hell. Stripped to the waist with sweat rags girdling their necks were about eight or more men digging into a mountain of coal, scooping it into large shovels with extra long handles and rushing four or more at a time to feed the cavernous fiery mouths of the five huge furnaces that crackled and spat ferociously with each succeeding shovelful. Serving merely, it would seem, to wet their enormous appetites. Everything in the place seemed almost black contiguous with the yawning furnaces. The Faustian scene was further exemplified by the appearance of the men who were covered from head to foot in black coal dust, with their eyes glowing red. Some of them wore sweat rags around their noses and mouths for the purpose of keeping out the coal dust, but most washed the dust down with their tea. Making tea for the gang was Jack's first job as soon as he arrived.

The work carried out by these men called for more than the average grit, although hungry wives and children were often the spirit and a better alternative to the dole queues and the degradation that this entailed. As it was, they considered in the circumstances that they were the favored few, for it was the fact that of being in the know and getting one's name at the top of the waiting list, that one was able to land a job.

The next problem was holding the job. It was Bill's second week with the company and he had been shown by the others not to face the searing flames of the oven head on, but always sideways and being right handed he had already learned to throw the coal from that side. Now he must learn the tricks of being left hand handed which was more fraught with difficulties as he was to find out. He knew and faced up to the fact that he would have to suffer terrible pain before he could master the job. The team tried their best to make it easy for a new man and this was what Jack was doing making the tea at the beginning of the shift, instead of starting straight away on the furnaces.

The job paid a bare wage, which did not allow for

luxuries of any kind. The terrible heat sapped their energy at a fast rate and it took only one man not pulling his weight to put a burden on the rest. So about a fortnight was considered sufficient time for hardening up. There was, however an indefinable 'spirit' among these East End people, which was to manifest itself to the world in the war which was soon to come. It was something, although tenuous, call it spirit if you like, which was handed down from one generation to another. One could truly label them a courageous people.

Chapter II

Milly built up a fire in the grate. Taking an old woolen shawl off the hook on the kitchen door, she wrapped it around her. Then, sitting in a chair, her father had not long vacated, began to read a book. The fire had to be kept going all night for the cold night air brought racking coughs from Ted. Dozing on and off, Milly kept the room temperature constant while tending to the sick boy. Hardly had she settled down, when her mother called her. Not liking to venture at this late hour into the inky blackness of the hall, she lit a candle. The drafty hall seemed suddenly to come to life with goblins as the flames licked the cold night air. Shivering, she pulled the shawl tightly around her shoulders as she reached the staircase that led to the upstairs flat inhabited by Paddy O'Neil and his family - the former usually bringing his compatriots home for a round of drinks after the local pub had closed. But tonight was the night before payday, so money was scarce.

Milly entered the room opposite the staircase. "Take Janie and put her into the chair by the fire. Then go a few doors and fetch old Mrs. Macintosh. Tell her the pains have started, don't forget the key to get back in again." Aunt Rose came from next door along with her sister in-law. All disappeared into the bedroom. Wide awake now I thought I would join them, but the burly midwife angrily shooed me away. "Go, wait in the other room child, your brother or sister won't be long now."

The thrill of seeing our baby brother was a sight Milly and I never forgot. I was a little disappointed at not having seen the stork that was supposed to fetch him. Ted was too sick to realize that he was now the elder brother.

Chapter III

Milly always helped me to cross the roads and then she would leave me to make my own way back home. I did not mind this, for I had a secret I thought no one knew about.

One day when I was standing outside the gates leading into an old church, an old woman stepped in front of them. Opening the gate, she went along the path and up the worn steps leading to a large heavy door. Opening it, she stepped inside. Always given to curiosity, I followed in close behind. On entering the church I was struck by the all pervading darkness of the place. I was stirred by the sight of a large shining cross. When my eyes became accustomed to the inner darkness of the place I felt as though I was in a kind of fairyland. There were lighted candles round the cross and various other places, which created an aura of mystery and otherworldliness. Never before had I seen such magnificent flowers during winter; the sight overwhelmed me.

This now became my secret. Every day, after school, I would enter the church, and sitting in one of the pews, let its quietude and beauty enter into me. Sometimes it would be full of people, but most times it was empty. In my mind, although I was not aware of it, there was an intuitive perception of the unknown, which was to manifest itself in one form or another with the sinuous passage of time. At these fleeting moments of childhood awareness, I was fascinated by it.

Chapter IV

Dawn showed itself to be one of those rare November days, just as if spring had decided to pay a visit to see how people were coping with winter. The rows upon rows of chimney pots, appeared to act like sentinels, guarding the sleeping people beneath them, as they stood to attention in the light breaking the darkness.

Victoria had risen early, having been unable to go back to sleep after giving George his early morning feed. She now felt as if she had sat longer than she had intended. It was a code of honor that the fronts of houses should gleam from as early in the day as possible. Today being Saturday, it was nine o'clock before the doors were opened and brass tins, dusting cloths were placed on the doorstep ready for use. The coconut fiber door mats were beaten against the iron railings that skirted each house. If anyone took the time to examine them they could not fail to observe their peculiar uniqueness, in that they resembled misplaced Gothic pretentious quaintness of a bygone age. The tops of the railings terminated in points as if urging one to look up into the sky. But, as was usually the case, people's heads were bent low to their work. It was only the kids who walked along the iron ledge – clutching the spikes one by one, finishing up at the other end of the street, who ever took the trouble to look up.

Chapter V

The unexpected sunshine felt good for the children and before long the games of summer were in full swing - games such as hopscotch, knuckle-bones, hoops, whip and top, just plain chasing and fighting too. Also cashing in on the fine weather were the various sorts of street entertainer, one of whom was now making his way down Plinters Street. The music blared as the old man turned the handle of the organ, and a mangy looking monkey started to perform his set tricks. Girls danced in a circle round the old man and his monkey. The boys tapped their feet, and vied with one another at whistling. After a while the old man stopped the music. The monkey then pulled a greasy old hat off his master's head and went among them for donations of money. Many ran indoors to beg halfpennies from their parents, for although they were poor themselves, well, they remembered that most of the street entertainers were themselves returned servicemen, who could often boast the rank of officer. Being the first entertainer on the scene, he was also the luckiest for as the day wore on, the number of donations diminished.

Chapter VI

Through the countless chimneys came the red departing arrow rays of the setting sun. They fell and danced in a myriad of colors on the copper and tin saucepans, vases, china plates and other wares. This was the last barrow hawker of the day. It was a good thing for him that money was not exchanged for his goods, for it was ragged he was after – and he let it be known far and wide, "Any old rags, any old rags. Come and see what I've got for you ladies."

Victoria gave way to my entreaties - "There's a lot of goldfish. "Two goldfish coming just for you young lady." said the gentleman with the shifty eyes. They had seemed enormous viewed through the vendor's bowl. Now transferred to my tiny jam jar, the fish looked pathetic; in fact I could barely see them. There were cries all round, "Stop cheating the kids. Why for a bundle that size, you could well let 'er 'ave one of them there goldfish bowls, why don't yer mate." There were murmurs of assent all round. Furtively he eyed the bundle of clothes, "Break me yer will. 'Ere take this." He then began to light the candles in his barrow lamps. Very soon he disappeared from the scene as darkness fell.

The lamplighter man was on his way down the street, lighting the lamps as he went. He reached the one outside the Reynolds; proudly clutching my newly acquired bowl of goldfish, I stood watching him. The man was holding a long pole in his hand, on which, somewhere near the top was a large hook. On the extremity was a wick, held in place by a wire. He pulled on the two chains that hung from the rather ornate iron and glass lamp shade, with the hook, and holding the lighted wick a short way from the very fragile gas mantles, caused them to pop and sizzle as they slowly turned from red to white hot as the gas caught. He, then by pulling the chain on the opposite side, adjusted correctly the amount of gas being fed in, then moved on to the next lamp.

I went indoors and stood the goldfish bowl on the table next to the couch, in full view of Ted. Bill was drinking a cup of tea before going off to work. Milly asked me for a hand in folding the napkins, while mum fed George.

All was quiet now on Plinters Street, except for the faint sizzling, or hissing sound given off by the gas lamps, which cast their eerie glow into the shadows of the night.

Chapter VII

Bill pulled his worn overcoat round his lean frame as he closed the door of the retort building behind him. He stood for a moment with his face raised to the gently falling snowflakes, which melted on impact, creating miniature streams threading their way through the dry broken skin.

The task before him now was not a pleasant one. It was a fair distance from the gasworks to his mother in law's home. She lived on the top floor of a block of flats the first of their kind in the district. On reaching the building, Bill entered the wide opening and stood looking up at the never ending concrete spiral stairs. Wearily he began the long ascent. He was resting for a while on the landing before the last flight when the door on the right opened up, crashing against the inside wall. Painful yelps from a puppy, were accompanied by roars from a huge man, who filled the doorway with his frame. A squirming furry bundle held in one hand, was being hammered by the other. At the sight of this cruelty, anger welled up in Bill. Words came to mind, but were unutterable; as extreme dryness of the throat prevented the emission of any sound. The man soon became aware of Bill's presence, which had the adverse effect of amplifying his violence towards the little animal. After first trying to defend his actions, "You should see the mess she's made." The tone of his voice defied an answer, but Bill contained his anger, as the man became more aggressive and made as if to attack him too. But Bill was ready for him. Suddenly, a crafty grin spread over his face. He placed the trembling animal on the floor and straightening up, looked down on the victim, as if from a great height, "Poor thing, poor little thing," he said. Then, with the alacrity of a skilled football player, he kicked the animal with such force as to send it past where Bill was standing, and down a further flight of stairs, where it lay as dead. "She's all yours mate." He slammed the door shut.

With little hope of finding the puppy alive, Bill went back down the flight of stairs to where it was lying. He lifted up the limp form and was surprised to feel that the heart was still beating. Gently he felt over the rest of the body to find it had sustained three broken legs. Holding it like a baby in his arms, he continued up the two flights of steps, and knocked on the door of his mother-in-law. The foregoing incident had somehow enabled him to overcome his hesitancy about the favor he was about to beg.

When the door was opened, she showed surprise at seeing Bill standing there. It was seldom that he paid her a visit. She surmised that he was after something.

"Isn't that Mr. Lawson's puppy you've got there?"

"Was," Bill corrected.

As the small pleasant women went about the task of

making tea, Bill narrated the events of the past ten minutes. He then took wood from a bundle near the fire, and proceeded to make splints with which to set the animal's legs. "It's in good hands now," she said. Drinking his tea in silence, he turned the subject of his visit over in his mind, and wondered how he should broach it. Unconsciously she gave him a lead. "How are Victoria and the children?"

"She's fine, but the two girls have been sick. Ted still isn't strong and George never stops crying." He added half to himself.

"Oh," was all she said. Bill was beginning to feel his pride was at stake. He found himself asking her for a loan of some money to tide him over Christmas. He had been sick himself and had only just returned to work. He could arrange to pay her back in three or four weeks. She remained silent all the while, and he felt he could have bit his tongue out for the asking. They really didn't like each other very much. As if reading his thoughts, however, and knowing what it had cost him to ask this favor of her, she relented.

"About how much do you want Bill?" She spoke kindly, but in his mind, condescendingly. He flinched in anger, "Oh, a pound if you will spare it." She nodded, and turned her back on him, at the same time lifting up the front of her long black dress and several petticoats. Embarrassed, Bill walked over to the window and looked down on the street far below. He noticed a child standing near the edge of the nearby pavement. He was partly covered with falling snow, giving him the appearance of a miniature snowman. He appeared to be watching the window Bill was standing at. His thoughts were suddenly switched back to the unpleasant situation he was in, by his mother-in-law's voice. "Here's two pounds, now no nonsense about taking it. I've got all the lads working, except for Sid." He took the offered money, wondering as he did, just how lucky they all were having jobs in these hard times. He thought that after all he may have misjudged her.

"I'll pay you back as soon as possible during the new year," he said, as she was seeing him off. The puppy was now ensconced inside his jacket, having been restored with warm milk. The warmth of being close to his body very soon sent her to sleep.

Chapter VIII

Bill put his head round the children's bedroom door and poked faces at them. They loved this, for invariably, as they knew from past experience, this was a precursor to a forthcoming happy event. Victoria was putting the little knobs of coal left in the house with the fire; a worried frown was on her face. She turned at the laughter. Catching her eyes, he jerked his head in the direction of the kitchen, and disappeared down the hall. Following him, she feared the worst, but was surprised and happy that her mother had loaned so much. Now she could go down the road and buy some fish and chips. She smiled happily to herself, when a few minutes later she heard their delighted laughter coming from the bedroom. "Rose," that's what she'll call the puppy.

Chapter IX

Christmas Eve had arrived and the children begged to

go out to see the lights and decorations. A week had gone by since the doctor had pronounced them all to be well again. Doubts still existed as to Teds' condition, and it was agreed he should be confined to bed during the afternoon, and a warm scarf was to cover his nose and mouth when he was taken out with the family in the evening.

    Today being Saturday, Christmas Eve, the markets stayed open usually until about eleven o'clock in the evening. It was an entertainment in itself, this late night shopping, particularly at Christmas.

    Victoria was able to hand George over for the next few hours to Aunt Rose next door. Money was short, they were told as they closed the door behind them, so they had to watch their spending. It had been snowing very lightly, but had stopped. "Oh it would be lovely to have a white Christmas," said Ted. "Yes, Ted, It would be wonderful", I replied

    Plinters Street was dressed in its annual festival bunting and on each door hung a laurel wreath. The children were becoming excited and began eagerly to pull their mother forward into the tram queue. The trams ran right through the market place, which seemed to never end. It was thronged with people surging backwards and forwards in a moving, panorama of color and jubilant commerce, with shouts and calls of stall holders vying with each other for customers. Myriad colored lights were strung everywhere, even round the poles, which supported the tram wires. Heads were twisted at angles, one would have thought impossible to achieve. They were pushed along and jostled by the crowd which just kept going. Ted complained that he could not see very much, so his mother carried him for a short while. The children were delighted with the toys in the shop windows, and on the stalls. There were china dolls beautifully dressed; train sets, complete with carriages and wagons run by clockwork, set on rails, amongst scenic impressions of country and town, stations and goods yards; enormous boxes containing mechanics sets for building engineers and others mechanically minded. There were many kinds of games, jigsaw puzzles, racing cars, dolls houses, all too numerous to name. Teds' eyes lit up at the sight of them, but not wanting to dwell too long on the toy counters, Victoria urged them on. But there was no escaping. His eyes rested on a whole battalion of tin soldiers – which included the guards from Buckingham Palace. Milly could not be beyond noticing the degrees of affluence and poverty displayed before her young eyes.

God's creatures were not always "bright and beautiful," neither was grinding poverty which seemed to her mind, the lot of the average folk she saw around her. There were those she noticed, who were able to spend money without blinking an eye, bestowing on their children the most fabulous gifts beyond her wildest dreams. "Santa Clause" in her opinion, was not a just man, and that's all there was to it. Unlike Ted and Janie who lived in a dream world anyway, she knew all about Father Christmas.

Most of the traders wore checkered cloth caps on their head, and wore silk scarves tied round their necks. Some of the harder ones had taken off their coats and rolled up their shirt sleeves. Cigarettes and matchboxes stuck out from waist coat pockets, ready for a quick fag when there was a lull in trade. It was a joy to listen to the banter which passed between them and people who gathered in clusters round their stalls. Their laughter brought warm air into contact with cold air, causing miniature vapor trails to form little clouds rising over each stall. In the wan gaslight, people looked a pale green or perhaps a sickly orange. Everywhere, they appeared to be jostling frantically with one another to get close enough to see.

Milly and I, being small enough to slip though the throngs, were able to see the many interesting and beautiful wares on display. They were fascinated at one stall by the many colors emanating from lead crystal vases, bowls and candlesticks. Victoria called, and they moved on. At the next place they were both surprised and amused to see the owner, who was selling very large and well made towels, throw one on the ground and jump, leaving dirty marks from his boots on it and exclaiming as he did, "All right, break me, send me to the workhouse, you won't buy for two and six. Out they go to you my darlings, not for two shillings, or one and nine pence, or one and three pence, all I want for them is a shilling." It took a strong hand on the purse not to be tempted to buy willy-nilly.

Victoria bought a few things for the children's Christmas stockings, while Milly took care of Ted and I. All the while, the pearly King and Queen, shining like the moon, with thousands of pearl buttons of all sizes sewn on their clothes had a crowd clapping their hands, while they danced in the middle of the road bringing the traffic to a standstill. The Bobby in charge moved them on, good naturedly smiling at their comments about policemen.

Two pennies bought a large carton of delicious jellied eels, as only the East End cockney could cook them. Many warmed their hands by the coke fires, whose owners vended roasted chestnuts. The popping of the skins told when they were cooked. They were placed into brown paper bags while still very hot and this was an added boon in keeping one's hands warm.

Too soon it was over. The girls returned a bundle of

second hand comics, bought for a farthing, held tightly in their hands. James had acquired a small dented toy lorry from a stall owner with more insight than a learned academic. He had seen that look on the boy's face. Victoria purchased a carton of jellied eels for Jack. She tasted one, just to make certain that they were fresh. A large bag of cheaply bought grocery, gave every indication that a good Christmas dinner would be held tomorrow.

Milly stayed up to help fill the gaily colored net stockings which were to be hung over the mantelpiece, to be found by the children the following morning, which was Christmas day. They contained apples, nuts, oranges, paint books, boxes of paints, fun hats and balloons. Some brightly colored glass bracelets for the girls, a tool set for Ted, and gloves for Bill. George was to get a rubber Donald Duck, and some jelly babies, and Rose, the family's newly acquired pup, a collar. She was at present asleep in the corner of the kitchen in a small box the family had provided for her. Her legs were healing well and she was becoming devoted to her new owners. So Christmas began happily, if not rich, for the Reynolds family.

Chapter X

The old year departed and the New Year arrived with the wailing of ship's sirens and the peeling of church bells. It was the tradition to open one's doors to allow the tall, dark stranger (usually invisible!) to cross the threshold, bringing with him good luck for the New Year.

Unfortunately, no such dark stranger crossed the Reynolds threshold this time, for Mr. Reynolds had hurt his back at work the day before, and Teds' health had taken a turn for the worse. Victoria decided to get a 'specialist' to have him examined. Without consulting Bill, she went to Woolworth's the following day and purchased a sixpenny wedding ring, making sure at the same time, the girl at the counter could see the ring she was already wearing, for she did not want her jumping to wrong conclusions about her. Once outside, she quickly slipped her wedding ring off, and substituted the Woolworth's product. She noticed how very light it was by comparison. She would get another ring some day she was sure. Slipping into the nearest jewelry shop, she inquired how much she would get for the ring. She did not have to haggle for long, for the kindly old Jew, sensing her distress, settled a fair price on the ring. It was just enough to pay the fees of a specialist.

Chapter XI

Doctor Hadley, it seemed, had problems of his own. Being a man dedicated to his work among the impoverished people of London, his surgery was very often overcrowded, necessitating long hours and late closing. He would sometimes be up most of the night, making calls on the very sick of the neighborhood, or for maternity cases. He had a partner, his wife. She had taken to drinking when their only son had been killed on a cycle one day, on his way back from school. Her drinking had been largely instrumental in causing him to move away from a more affluent circle of friends and acquaintances. That had been fifteen years ago. It was put around, and generally believed, that his wife was slowly dying from alcohol poisoning.

He was that moment reprimanding a middle aged woman in his room. Suddenly, the door was flung open, and a protesting, weeping woman was unceremoniously shown out. "I'm sick of listening to your complaints, there's nothing wrong with you. Get out of my sight, get out!"

He was a man of about sixty, with hair sparsely adorning his head. Now closing the door firmly behind him, he sat for a moment behind his desk, in order to marshal back his self control before seeing the next patient - man due to go in next got up and left. This puts Victoria next in the queue. She wondered how she would be received, but she had little reason to fear, for the doctor had calmed himself considerably when her turn for seeing him had come. After consulting him about her son's condition, and the desire to get a specialist to see him, he informed her that he would call at her home later as soon as arrangements to this effect could be made.

On reaching home that evening, Victoria placed the money from the sale of the ring in a small cardboard box which she buried under the household linen. She paused to take a look at herself in the mirror. All things considered, she supposed, one couldn't complain. Bill has proven himself a good husband and father. Climbing on to a chair, she opened a small white box located high on the wall, he had nailed it there to be out of the way of the children. Reaching inside she took out a bottle of liniment and made her way to the kitchen. She stood the bottle in warm water to take the chill off before rubbing the contents on her husband's back. It was now very quiet in the house, signifying the fact that the children must now be asleep. She cast a look at Ted and felt a great sense of relief that something positive could at last be done for him

Chapter XII

Crocuses opened to the watery sunshine. One front garden had an abundance of them - I looked round to see if anyone was watching, then moved inside the gate, and began picking my favorite colors, counting to six, when a loud banging on a window startled me. Looking up from my small height, I saw that the lace curtains were parted. A distorted angry visage accompanied by a violently waving arm, told me that my presence on those precincts was far from welcome. I took off immediately through the gate, and ran down the road, feeling like a hunted criminal. Pausing for a while to get my breath back, and seeing that no one was following, I began to walk with one leg on the curb and the other in the gutter. That's how I saw the penny. Picking it up, I turned it over and around, noting with a thrill, the date on the coin. It was as old as I was, soon I would be eight. I'll spend it on my birthday; I thought to myself.

"Mummy, I've got something for you," she called from the hall.

"I'm in here," Victoria called from the kitchen.

 She saw what I was holding in my hands. "They're lovely dear, just beautiful." She refrained from asking her where she obtained the flowers, which were usually wild, but in this case a tame variety, and defiantly purloined from some garden. Skipping into her bedroom, I placed the penny among my

Sunday school texts. But it played on my mind, by Saturday lunchtime I felt compelled to spend it.

Chapter XIII

The corner shop with its funny slanting windows looked as if it smiled at one. It spilled over with wares of many kinds; scrubbing brushes, tin baths, buckets and brooms. Bundles of wood on the pavement just outside. Inside on the left was chickenfeed held in deep sloping boxes. There were nails of every size, also ropes and chains. Just inside on the right stood a high counter, fenced in at the top, except for a small gap, where an extra large sloping glass ashtray, oblong in shape and having a dip in the center, was used for the exchange of money for the goods, which were handed over the counter. It was a post office come general shop. Further down, a low counter ran the full length of the shop, where huge rounds of cheese stood cut in halves. I went over to look at one. It was a seething mass of little white worms, curling and twisting, some knocking into each other and falling onto the counter and the floor below. Picking one up, to idly watch its futile struggle in the palm of my hand; I joined the short queue by the door.

When it was my turn to be served, I reached up and placed the penny in the ashtray. Just as I did this, a youth pushed me aside, asking for a packet of cigarettes. He paid for them and hurriedly left the shop. Feeling abashed at this unwelcome intrusion, I asked for three sherbet draws, licorice straps, and some jelly babies. Mr. Chandler held the goods in his hands as if waiting for something.

"That will be one penny, Janie."

"I put it in the dish Mr. Chandler." He shook his head disbelievingly, "I put it there before a man pushed in front of me." Mr. Chandler shook his head impatiently,

"You're having me on Janie. I'll tell your father about this." Behind me, people in the queue were becoming impatient. Red in the face, and near to tears, I stood my ground,

"I put the penny in the dish," I claimed.

At that moment, dad walked into the shop. It was usual for him to make small purchases of leather of a Saturday morning for mending the family's shoes. Mr. Chandler beckoned to him.

"Come here a moment Bill, will you." He came over and saw me standing there.
"Hello Janie, what are you doing here?" Before I had the opportunity to say anything, the shopkeeper was already muttering something in his ear. Dad looked down at me quizzically,
"Janie, just what are you up to? I want the truth now, mind you."
"But dad, I put the money there, honest I did." he shook his head, paid for the sweets and handed them down to me, saying as he did, "Always the truth Janie, always the truth." I shook my head in anger and with tears running down my face, veritably blinding me, I ran out of the shop, making to cross the road.

There was a screeching of brakes, as a car came rapidly to a stop, but not before knocking her over. Darkness came over her, but was aware of shouts and a sea of faces coming and going.

"Thank God," someone murmured as she opened her eyes. "She's only grazed, although there's a lump rising on her forehead."

"Missed going under the wheels by a fraction – she's lucky she's not dead." The sherbet draws lay spilt on the road as Bill had rushed to stop her from running in front of the oncoming car.

Janie was carried home, given an aspirin and put to bed. Bill later inquired of Victoria, had she given Janie the penny? She shook her head; how could we afford it anyway. You have been back to work only a week, and already we're a week behind with the rent. He agreed, but remained silent.

After dinner, he got on with mending the shoes. "Never be down on your uppers," he was often heard to say. "Down on your uppers, down on your luck." Watching his face, Milly could fathom that he was still very upset by the events of the afternoon. This wasn't the first time Janie had lied, he thought. Yet he could not understand her being so upset, particularly as he had undertaken to buy her the sweets in the end. He went quietly into the bedroom to look at her. It had all been too much, she was lying fast asleep.

Chapter XIV

The giant Victorian building towered over the surrounding shops and warehouses. Its bleakness cast a gloom over the two girls hurrying towards it. A pealing bell loudly proclaimed the time. They started to run. Entering the grounds of the building, they heard the sound of hymn singing in progress. They entered the gloomy interior of the building and turned in the direction of the headmistress's office. They joined the long queue waiting outside. Morning prayers were over, and hundreds of children have now filed back to their classrooms, some glancing at the latecomers, some smiling, others serious, but glad all the same that it wasn't them among the already long queue of malefactors.

The headmistress emerged from her office, and proceeded to walk slowly past the children lined up outside. They knew from past experience that she was counting them. She then continued with her measured pacing, up and down the line like a company sergeant major. She was a woman six feet tall, exceedingly lean, the bones of her rib cage almost revealed through a thin, but meticulously cleaned, white blouse. A hip bone protruded on either side of her very straight brown skirt, which reached almost to her ankles. Very dark rimmed glasses gave her that extra sternness of visage. Janie and Milly, who were in the queue, nicknamed her Miss Murdstone. Miss Murdstone was every bit as cruel and unyielding as any one of Dickens' monsters.

A light sprang into her yellow speckled brown eyes as she looked up and down the line. Just then, two more late comers rushed to join them. She grabbed the clothes on their backs, and ran them back towards the school gates. "Home you both go. I'll let your parents deal with you. Don't come to school again if you can't get here earlier than this." Weeping, the children turned home to face angry parents.

Miss Murdstone was in good form this morning. After another silent appraisal of the shivering line of children - she loved a prolonged prelude, it excited her sadistic propensities to keener pitch - she fetched the cane from her office.

Many came away from the ordeal, crying with pain. They were jeered at by the more defiant ones as letting the side down. The line moved up slowly as punishment was meted out. Milly's turn came. "Mildred Reynolds I should have thought that you would have shown a better example to your class." She received extra punishment thereby for lowering her standard. Janie now stood looking up at her, her big beautiful; and almost far-seeing eyes fixed themselves onto the headmistress' eyes, taking her off guard for a brief moment. Then her face hardened, all glint of compassion disappearing. She felt enraged at displaying weakness. Janie, needless to say, obtained extra whacks. Tears sprang into her eyes, but she did her best to blink them away before they were noticed by others.

Few complaints ever found their way to parents about Miss Brown, as she was known, for such was the esteem she was held in around the district, that very few would ever have believed them.

Chapter XV

Rain had begun on the way to school that morning, which, by the end of the school day had transformed itself into a veritable deluge. The very small children, without big brothers or sisters to see them home, were held back in two classrooms. Milly took charge of Janie, and they raced for home. The rain beat relentlessly on them; hardly able to see ahead, nevertheless they forced themselves on. The gutters were full to overflowing. Black clouds enveloped the sky, turning day into partial night. Most traffic was virtually at a standstill. A lot of people were carrying torches, out looking for their children.

By the time the girls reached Plinters Street, the water was about level with Janie's waist. Milly hung on to the iron rails urging her on, up the ledge beside her. Gradually they found their way home. Victoria had been looking out of the window for them, and rushed to let them in. The water poured into the hall and it was a fight to close the door. It had not yet reached the height of the letter box in the door.

An hour later, when items of the floor of the flat had started to float, the sky suddenly showed blue, and the rain stopped as if by command. Amazingly the large drains coped with the water once the rain stopped, and by the time the work force from the city headed for home, the flood was well past. At least in Plinters Street, many homes would take days to dry out.

Mrs. O'Neil took Ted and George upstairs away from the damp conditions of the Reynolds flat on this rare occasion; she was more than glad she lived upstairs.

Tommy Fisher was talking to old Mrs. Kowaski, who was, as usual, sitting in her rocking chair engaged in her favorite past time of observing the saga of life unfolding, in all its gyrations and scintillations, within the prospect of her limited vision. Back and forth, she rocked. From under her old tweed cap, her beady eyes would miss nothing that went on around her. Clad in men's clothing, she wore a dirty old shawl around her shoulders and a pipe in her mouth. She displayed a large mole on her chin, from which grew long shaggy looking hairs. Only very inclement weather would keep her away from her 'observation' porch, where she commanded a full view of all that took place around her. No one knew her age; many could remember her sitting in the same place when they were young themselves.

Chapter XVI

Tommy stopped talking as he watched the Reynolds girls go by. A pretty picture they made in their dainty dresses and frilly bonnets, displaying rosebuds on either side. They were going to their Uncle Harry's wedding, and were chatting excitedly and laughing gaily, until their eyes fell on Tommy.

He was the bully of the street. Pretending not to notice him, they nodded to the old woman and hurried on their way to the bakery, where a large bag of iced cream pieces could be purchased for the price of two pence. They were to have these with a cup of tea before leaving for the wedding. Mr. Polly, the baker, put in a few of their favorite cakes, gratis, and went to the trouble of seeing them across the busy road.

Tommy, who had chosen to follow them, under the evil auspices of Mrs. Kowaski, had hidden himself from view of the now approaching girls. As they drew level with him, he jumped out in front of them. "Try to pass," he jeered.

"Get out of the way Tommy," ordered Milly. He continued to stand, his arms folded and legs outstretched, waiting for them to move.

"He can't chase us both," Milly whispered into Janie's ear. "I'll make a run for it, and you can take the cream slices back home as fast as you can." She began to run, and Tommy Followed her, but then he suddenly changed his mind as he saw Janie running for home. Although she was a fast runner, his very long strides soon enabled him to catch up with her. Twisting away from him, she caught her foot in the curb causing her to spill the cakes, some of which got under her shoes, making her slip and fall. As she fell, she hit her head on the edge of the iron railings. The blood flowed from the open cut in a crimson stream down on to her new white dress.

The sight of blood scared him; he took to his heels and very quickly disappeared from the scene. Mrs. Kowaski hadn't missed a thing, and as the bully came running past, she shot out her, large, thick cane with alacrity hard to credit for her great age, and brought him down with a resounding thud. He howled in pain. She opened her toothless mouth and rocked back and forth in silent laughter.

Milly, on returning, was horrified at the sight of her sister. A man passing picked her up and carried her home. He offered to fetch the doctor, while Bill, who was irate over Janie's condition, went in search of Tommy Fisher. But it was a little while before he could catch up with him and give him a telling off he deserved. Victoria bathed the wound. Fortunately, it was superficial.

They attended the wedding, but there was no pretty dress for Janie. How unheeding life seems at times, as yet another day passed away in Plinters Street. I looked up at the stars that night and fell to wondering how they could appear so callous to the affairs of mankind.

It was Monday. A hard day's work ahead of her, Victoria sorted the colors from the whites, placed the rubbing board in the large sink of hot water and the blue bag for rinsing the whites on the ledge above the sink. Soap in hand, she proceeded to place a shirt against the board, simultaneously rubbing the garment up and down, and alternately immersing it in water, when there came a single knock at the door. One knock was an indication that it was for downstairs. A terrible unexplained feeling of anxiety welled up from the pit of her stomach, causing her heart to race. There had been something ominous in the knock. Pulling herself together and drying her hands, she went to open it.

Dr. Hadley stood on the step. Bidding him good morning, she invited him in. "I won't keep you long Mrs. Reynolds, but I must warn you before I say anything, that the news about your son is not good. I have just received the report back from the specialist, which I have here. He has diagnosed tuberculosis. Apparently, he has a large spot on both lungs. But fortunately at this stage of the illness, there is a good measure of hope, if you could either have him placed in a sanitarium, or you yourself take him away from the city to a place where he can have access to fresh air and good wholesome fresh food. I should very much advise the latter course, but I can see in your case that I shouldn't have to give this advice. I hope, Mrs. Reynolds; that things will work out for you. There is nothing like the healing love of a close-knit family, such as yours." Asking her to keep in touch, Dr. Hadley quickly saw himself out.

Victoria was silent, when later on the girls asked her had she been crying. That night, she and Bill held a long discussion. Thursday came. The children noticed her eyes were still red and quite swollen. Uncle Dan, Auntie's Rose and May and other relations came round that evening. From their bedrooms, they could hear the low and anxious murmuring of voices till quite late in the evening. Milly spoke her troubled thoughts, "Wonder what's wrong? Why does everyone seem so unhappy?" Both girls tossed restlessly in their sleep.

Next morning, however, the flat was unrecognizable. All the items that made home, were packed in cardboard boxes and plywood tea chests. The hall seemed darker and undignified without its hallstand. All the beds were dismantled, and mattresses stood up against the walls. "What's happening mum?" they inquired. Victoria shook her head and refused to answer.

After school that day, I went into the church to pray for Ted, who I knew was now very ill. I lit a candle as I had seen others do, and knelt in front of the shining cross. "God, I don't know where you are, or if you can hear me, but please make my brother better, coz he's very sick and mum keeps crying, amen. Janie rose and made her way to the back pew, thinking she and 'God' were all alone in the church.

A priest got up from one of the pews, and made his way down the aisle. A short distance down, he genuflected and turned to walk towards the door. He stopped where Janie sat, and looked down at her, just as she looked up at him. He made the sign of the cross over her head. Surprised, she looked more closely at his face, wondering why he looked so sad. Without a word the priest turned round and continued on his way out. Janie watched until the door closed behind him.

Chapter XVII

That night they slept on mattresses on the floor. Their cousins from next door were allowed to join them. This gave them the opportunity to play games so they rolled head over heels and engaged in pillow fights, as the circumstances were tinged with no small measure of novelty and not a little excitement, no one seemed to mind.

They were however, a little put out and surprised, to be woken up in the early hours of the morning, and have their mattresses pulled from under them.(This was called the moonlight flit, as people often left their "obode" without paying the rent.) The front door was wide open, and two strange men were putting the last items of furniture into the lorry, which stood outside. Cocoa and biscuits were handed round and much kissing and handshaking took place among the relatives. Bill assisted Victoria on to the back of the lorry, where the mattresses had been placed. Ted seemed small and lost in the blanket, as he was gently placed in her arms. Milly then climbed in, and George was put beside her. Janie took charge of Rose, the pup, and the goldfish bowl was placed in a large tin can. The back flap was bolted into place and last goodbyes whispered. Bill climbed into the front seat to give directions in the journey ahead. The lorry began to move slowly away.

"Where are we going mummy?" asked Janie.

"We are going to live in the country until Ted gets better. The doctor advised it." They all began to cry. It was a cold winter's morning, and they felt very tired and depressed.

After about an hour's ride, they found they were leaving the suburbs of London behind them.

"This is your brother's last chance," said Victoria.

"The man in the moon must be sorry for him too, coz

he's been following us all the way, and playing at hiding-go-seek in the clouds." said Janie

This brought laughter from Victoria and Milly, and they both wiped their eyes dry. It was a long way to Laindon Hills, where Aunt Grace lived, for the way was winding.

Chapter XVIII

Greetings from Aunt Grace and Uncle Max seemed to be lost in the concern shown for Ted. It was decided that someone be dispatched to fetch the local doctor, who was said to live about three miles away. They were sorry that they had not thought to detain the lorry which brought them. Max and Bill decided to set out together. Hardly a word passed between the two men, as they half ran, half trotted the three miles together.

Old Mrs. Williams, the doctor's housekeeper, took her time in answering the doorbell. Her head placed to one side, and hand to one ear bespoke partial deafness. Both were so much out of breath they could hardly speak as they tried to make her understand them. The general commotion brought the doctor to the door, who, sensed the urgency of the situation. Returning to his room, he donned an overcoat over his pyjamas, and grabbed his large black bag from the surgery. They followed him from the house. "We can talk on the way," he said, opening the car door for them to get in.

Very soon they were rattling their way over grass tracks and stony roads. Nodding his greetings to Grace as she opened the door, Doctor Punjab went straight over to where Victoria sat. She was holding the sick boy in her arms. He did not make her put him down, but knelt on the floor and gently unwrapped the blanket. "A hospital job," he said, but noticing the involuntary protective tightening of her arms around the child, added, "But between us, we'll do our best to pull him through the next few days. The change of air will have an effect on him, we hope for the better."

They all looked gratefully into his very brown understanding face. Bill cleared his throat, "Doctor, I haven't any money at the moment to pay you." A large brown hand came down upon his shoulder,

"It will be payment enough for the child to live. If you're any good at growing vegetables, Mrs. Williams would always welcome a few." Bill did not trust himself to reply. He walked with the doctor back to the car.

"I have given him an injection; he should sleep for a while. You must remind your wife to keep a constant check with the mirror. It must be held in front of the nose and mouth. If it clouds over, you can be assured that he is still breathing. If there is any change, I must be notified at once. Meanwhile, you should get some rest yourself, you look all in. I'll call again this evening."

Bill did not enter the cottage straight away, but stood listening to the noise of the receding car. Reaching for a small tin in his waistcoat pocket, he opened it and extracted a wafer thin cigarette paper and put it to his moist bottom lip where it hung, as he began scraping the last of the tobacco he had left between his fingers. Rolling it expertly, he placed the finished article into his mouth. Cupping his hands and striking a match, he quickly lit the cigarette, drawing deeply on it.

Absentmindedly, he watched the match splutter and die out in the crisp morning air. Drawing again, he stood looking over the rooftops of the few bungalows in the village below. Virgin land covered by small bushes and elm trees, spread out as far as the eye could see.

He looked at the cottage as he approached it. He liked what he saw; it seemed an oasis, with its flowerbeds, vegetable garden and fruit trees. Had anyone been observing him at that moment of time, they may have noticed, that in spite of everything, there was a definite spring to his step which was in tune with the season, as he walked towards the back door.

Chapter XIX

The train ground noisily to a stop at Laindon Hills Station. The two men, breathless with running, boarded it and sat down gratefully, as the guard blew the whistle for the train to move out. Bill chided him, "Thought you said your clock was fast."
"It was," claimed Max, "The blooming train must have been early." Max was a man of few words. As soon as he was relaxed, he pulled out a book and immediately lost interest in his surroundings. Bill changed to the seat opposite, which was empty, and lay down, dozing off and on, as the train pulled in and out of many stations on its way to London's Fenchurch Street Terminus.

At last his turn came to alight, and bidding his silent companion farewell, he joined other passengers on the way to the exit. Max got off and joined the jostling queues outside for the buses. They were trolley buses which ran this route. They were joined by what looked like long poles to overhead lines, sometimes causing violet colored flashes of light as they moved, and disconnecting themselves if a driver rounded a corner too quickly.

On this occasion with Max on the bus, a disconnection occurred outside one of the large co-operative stores. A few women pressed eagerly against the window panes, they had previously purchased groceries at one of these stores and were given coupons and a book to put them it.

"What's free this week?" a scrawny looking women was heard to ask her companion, whose face was seen to be pressed up hard against the bus window.

"A set of seven saucepans for two full books of coupons," she answered without taking her eyes off the ones displayed in the store windows.

"I need another five coupons to make two books," the scrawny woman rose beautifully to the occasion.

"I'll give you five from my book." She was unaware of the smug look of satisfaction which passed over the other woman's face.

Meanwhile, the bus conductor had drawn a long, tapering bamboo pole from its attachment under the bus, and looking like an ant carrying many times its own weight, staggered from side to side, backwards and forwards, becoming cross eyed and cross legged, in his efforts to hook the very distant pulleys back on to the lines. All the while, he was watched by driver and passengers alike, and finally greeted by cheers and bravos as he finally achieved his goal. Returning the pole to its position under the bus, he climbed back on board, revealing a large grin on his face. He felt good; he was indeed getting better at it. "Fares please, any more fares," he shouted. He began pushing his way through the overcrowded bus.

    The bus came to a halt outside the sugar refinery, where Max was to spend the next eight hours of his time. Many of the passengers got off here, leaving the bus comparatively empty. Max pushed through the gates, joining the moving sea of humanity, in his efforts to gain his work place. He reached it and clocked on, just as the wailing siren announced it was eight o'clock – time to start work. Hanging his coat on a hook beside him, he donned a pair of ex-army dungarees. He buttoned them up, without uttering a word to those around him. Picking up a large steel implement, he began to scrape the thick sticky black molasses which clung to the inside of a large vat, almost disappearing inside, as he tried to gather as much as he could into several clean tins, for himself and a few men he worked with, to take home. It was a popular spread for the children, as well as an excellent laxative. He set aside a larger tin for himself as he now had the Reynolds family living with him. It also entailed the added inconvenience of carrying it to the Technical Institute, where he attended evening classes after a day's work in the factory. He was keen to get out of the rut he was in, for, with a better education, there were opportunities within the firm.

    He was a descendant from a white Russian Jewish family, who in company with many hundreds of others, had to flee from Russian persecution, many years ago. These people upheld the traditions of furthering their education either at school, or later in life. They were also mostly trained opportunists, this trait being inculcated into them from an early age. The philosophy of education and opportunity, was ingrained into him, he considered the effort required in furthering his education after gruelling day's work, well worth his while. Very often, it would be eleven o'clock in the evening before he alighted from the train, for his long walk home.

Tonight, however, Bill Reynolds was even later. Unfortunately, he had lost the return half of his ticket, and was asking the ticket inspector at the gate to pass him. He refused to listen when Bill told him that he would have to walk the twenty miles or more home. When he finally limped into the cottage, it was past two in the morning. His first concern was for his son, and he brightened up considerably on being informed of an improvement in health. He took his position for the night, lying on the floor in front of the fire and dropped off into a deep sleep as soon as his head touched the pillow.

Chapter XX

"We can't stay here; it isn't fair to Brenda and Egan, taking their rooms." Victoria looked across at her sister as she spoke; they were making Teds bed.

"We can put you up for a few weeks longer. The doctor's calling tomorrow – let's ask him if the boy's well enough to be moved to another house. He's certainly brightening up, isn't it wonderful having him sit up like that after being so ill." He smiled at them both as they lifted him from his chair to put him back to bed again. His brother George stood holding himself up by the bedclothes, clambering to get in beside him.

"Let him mum," said Ted. "I'll show him how to colour

his paint book." Victoria relented,

"Well then, only for a short while. You mustn't tire yourself out though."

Both women left the bedroom, taking care to leave the door open, so they could see into the bedroom while having morning tea. The conversation was continued between the two, as they felt they had something to thrash out. "I really should look for a place to live," continued Victoria. Grace thought for a while before replying.

"Look, I know the district pretty well, and know most of the land agents. There could be some houses for letting, and I'll make it my business to see a few as soon as I've finished my tea." Victoria looked gratefully across at her sister, who was the eldest of nine children in the Holder family. Most of them were grown up, and four were already married. Looking at the two women sitting there, one would not have taken them for sisters. Grace had the dark colouring of her father's hair, and his dark brown eyes. In temperament too they were entirely different. Grace had not her sister's calmness of manner, but was quick to anger. She was, however, always prepared to help other people when she could. When the family were gathered together, one could not fail to see that common likeness, a feature to them all, namely large expressive soul searching eyes.

For the rest of the day, Grace undertook her search for a dwelling place for the Reynolds. Some of the houses she viewed were fairly large and spacious, but high rents, others were in poor condition. It was becoming late in the day. When feeling quite depressed, she decided for no apparent reason, to cross a field which leads to the back of Bamford's store. The lane in front of it wound its way up very high hills on the right, then made a steep descent to the township, five miles away to the left. She decided, while she was there, to purchase a few items, then left the store to make her way home.

　　　She noticed, as she walked out, in a front garden opposite, a large old tree, with a weather-beaten notice attached to it. The chipped red letters read 'To let'. Looking beyond the tree, she thought she liked the look of the double bay windowed bungalow, standing in the large overgrown garden. She crossed over and came to a small gate. Opening it, she made her way down the path towards the front door. Hanging from the eaves, just in front of the door, supported by two rusty chains, was a large emblem in faded gold lettering, which read, 'Bogner Regis'. Following the path round the house to the back, she came to a large patio. All over the back garden was displayed a wilderness of weeds mixed up with a variety of shrubs. She noticed some splendid looking roses, bravely thrusting their half formed buds to the light of the sun. A badly broken fence gave views all round of fallow meadows, with cows grazing on them. She noticed an extreme contrast in the garden to the right, which although beautifully set out and cultivated, gave her the impression of a certain military attachment on the part of the owner, with its unbending lines of shrubberies and vegetable gardens. A large old dog was lying by his kennel watching her, she thought, with only little interest, for after having given a few perfunctory barks, and feeling that he had done his duty, he was content to lie there, without moving it seemed, for the rest of the day. She could not descry the occupants, and assumed that they were either away or inside. Seeing a high narrow shed, she walked towards it, knowing that it must be the outside toilet. After struggling with some very tall and unyielding weeds, she managed to open the door, but soon shut it very quickly again, albeit, not before catching sight of the broken roof. She had the same problem where she lived, they were still not connected to the sewer.

Feeling pleased with her find, she turned down the path which lead to the lane, and hurried home. The children were round the table having their evening meal, when she arrived back. She drew Victoria into the kitchen, where they spoke excitedly together. "I'll not be able to pay a week's rent on it till Bill gets his pay on Friday," said Victoria.

"You go tomorrow and look at the house. If you like it, I'll loan you the money until Bill gets his pay. The rent shouldn't be more than twelve shillings. The owner's address is on the board in the front garden. Happy at the thought of living so close together, the sisters set down to dinner with the children.

Chapter XXIV

The day had mellowed by the time Doctor Punjab made his appearance at the cottage. Knocking on the back door, he opened it and walked in. The two women were busy ironing. They had not long washed the curtains, to put up in their new home, for the Reynolds were now the tenants. His teeth flashed white in contrast to his brown face, exposing his oriental charm, as he smiled at them on the way to the bedroom, wherein lay the sick boy. "When you have finished, you can come and do mine."
They groaned back at him, "We have done enough for one day, thank you Doctor."

"Well Ted," he said, as he entered the bedroom. "I must say, you are looking very well. Unbutton your jacket, I want to have a look at that big chest. Is there any pain now?"

"No Doctor," said Ted, his face brightening, for he had come to regard the doctor as his friend. After completing a thorough examination, he passed the stethoscope to Ted, and let him listen to his own heartbeats, and explaining in layman fashion, the operation of that all important pump. After making him button up his bed jacket, he put his hand into his bag and pulled out some of the boy's favourite sweets.

"Here's some bull's eyes for you Ted, now, you're not to eat them all at once," he admonished. "They should last until the next time I come and see you, which, let me see now, should be next Tuesday. Goodbye Ted, keep up the good work now."

Outside he faced Victoria's questioning eyes. "Yes, he is on the mend now Mrs. Reynolds. Build him up with good food, keep his room well aired, but make sure he's wrapped up warm. Cow's milk may be a bit strong for his condition, so I've arranged to have a goat delivered from Mr. Harrison's farm. It has been examined, and found to be grade one, by our veterinarian. He will continue making tests from time to time as he thinks fit. The rest is over to you Mrs. Reynolds."

Thanking him, she asked if Ted was well enough to be moved to their new home. Fires must be lit in all rooms to give them a thorough airing, before any attempt was made at moving him. Bidding them good evening, he left the house. On his way out, he noticed the other children absorbed in their various games. He waved a hand at them, hoping that very soon, young Ted would be able to join them.

Chapter XXI

Pulling old carrots up from the vegetable plot, the children were running down the path to feed them to Grumpy, a drag horse who was methodically chewing his way through the proffered food. Farmer Harrison had brought the goat, and was offering to take the Reynolds furniture while he was down that way. They very gratefully accepted his offer and many willing hands were now on the point of loading it into the large cart. Soon it was full, and they were ready to move, but not old Grumpy! He stood routed to the spot, peering through the long hair of his mane at the children, expecting more goodies. However, in the end he was forced to move, tho' very much against his will. The children were severely reprimanded for raiding Uncle Max's garden. Snorting with contempt, so it seemed to Janie, old Grumpy made off, dragging a fairly substantial load behind him. He was in the process of earning those ill gotten carrots. Slowly, he plodded over the uneven ground. The goat voiced her disapproval at being pushed into a corner. But it was not for long, for as soon as they reached Bognor Regis, she was staked out in the long grass.

    The pine wood fires in the grates sent their odours through the open doorway. As the furniture was brought in the children went running excitedly from room to room, but were eventually asked to play in the garden. Ted was placed in a chair next to the coal range. He could see through the window and watched the other children playing, feeding the goat. But soon they found it was more fun to chase each other round the bungalow. But after knocking into Uncle Max, they were told to confine their play to one quarter of the garden. Janie's cousin Brenda was the ring leader. It was she who decided to climb up a large tree, and along one of its branches, at the same time daring the others to follow her. Seeing them all grouped round the bottom of the tree, she immediately swung herself over the branch, hanging on by her hands. Soon she was in difficulties, as she apparently hadn't the strength of arm to swing back on to the limb again. Seeing this, they became alarmed, and called out for Uncle Max and Bill.

"Try to move down towards the tree trunk," said Bill. The ground was higher here, and as the branch sloped down, she could be reached if somebody jumped on the cart to assist her down. Farmer, Harrison, who had been watching had already backed the cart under the tree.

She refused to move, and just laughed at them. As Bill's anger mounted with her defiance, so she became more rebellious. He was finally able to get on to the branch, and inch his way toward her, feeling it creek and groan under the extra weight imposed on it. The group watched with bated breath, for even if they both fell in the cart, they would surely hurt themselves. But somehow he managed to grab her and draw her back to safety.
"Don't you ever do that again, young lady," shouted Bill angrily. She just laughed in his face, and poked her tongue out at him. Her father ordered an apology from her, but she ran off to the back of the garden, with some of the children following. From that moment, Bill developed an aversion for the child and she for him.
This episode dampened the happy spirit engendered by the moving to a new home, but after drinks and food had been served, it was soon forgotten. By the end of the day "Bognor Regis" was beginning to show signs of a happy and auspicious transformation, from dereliction, to homely domesticity, which bode well for the future. They all sat talking well into the night, cognizant of the fact, that by morning, they would all be tired out

Chapter XXII

Monday morning soon came. The two girls had been

enlisted at the local school, and cousins Brenda and Egan had arrived to show them the way. "Wish I could go to school," Ted called from his bedroom. Milly went to cuddle him. "Soon you'll be coming with us, you'll see." Victoria stood by the open door urging them to leave. She did not want them late on their first morning.

Rose seized the opportunity to rush past her and make towards the open gate. She followed them up the lane, but Janie brought her back again where she received a scolding. "Rose would have found her own way back home, now you must hurry Janie, or you'll be late."

They continued walking up the winding lane, then turned left onto a path, covered in large chipped stones, whose sharp edges pierced the soles of their shoes. Dad won't be pleased about this, thought Milly. They noticed several houses, some newly built, facing each other across the earth, which was deeply rutted by horse and cart tracks. There were no signs as yet, indicating street names, but most of the houses proclaimed theirs. Milly called them out as they passed each one, and choosing the ones they liked best.

At last they came to the school, which faced the main road running parallel to the lane which ran to the hills, at which point they joined together. They were surprised when they saw the small classrooms, which were laid out in circular formation, and mounted on wooden piles. Concrete pathways were seen to emanate from each, terminating in a quadrangular playing area, centrally situated.

A large gathering of children attracted by the newcomers, made a circle round them and began asking them questions. The situation was saved for them by the furious ringing of the school bell by one of the children. They all began to file in at the doors of their respective classrooms. As they stood to attention, a sportily middle aged man approached them, introducing himself as the headmaster. He ushered them into a small room in one of the buildings. After making them sit down, he placed several sheets of paper in front of them, in which were several questions and general knowledge, arithmetic and English. Milly applied herself to the task. Not so Janie, who gazed round the room, and out of the window, before bringing herself reluctantly to the task in front of her.

The headmaster returned later and examined their work. Milly's assessment placed her in the top of her class, while Janie had a fair idea where she would be placed. It was often said that if she took the trouble to apply herself, she could very easily make it to the top. But she was a daydreamer, who found learning a bore.

She was taken to Mr. York's class, and after a low murmuring between the two men, was placed at the desk behind the dunce of the class, which pleased him, but brought embarrassment to Janie, as the rest of the class begin to giggle.

Lunch time came not a moment too soon, but with no sign of Milly, but a bombardment of questions from the children around her. Only half a sandwich had been eaten, when the bell rang. As the afternoon dragged on, the teacher noticed Janie's inattention to her lessons and requested she read out 'loud and clear' from a passage in her English book. This pleased Janie. After all, hadn't she been trained by a music teacher to sing out loud and clear. She stood up proudly, book in hand, she would show them she was no dunce. Indeed, she spoke very well; the child to her left put her hands to her ears and suppressed a giggle. It caught like fire and soon all the class, joined by the teacher, were doubled up with laughter.

Poor Janie was near to tears, she knew she was good, and could see no reason for the laughter. The teacher, on recovering himself, looked half cynically at Janie, "When I said 'loud', I meant loud enough to be heard in this classroom, not over the whole school. We do not suffer from deafness!

What's your name?"

"Janie, Sir!"

"Janie is it. Will look to it Janie, you'd better pull your socks up smartly, I want a bit of learning out of you."

When the bell rang for home time, she was the first out of the classroom, but it did not end there. The two were followed by a gang of children, who on being let out of school, underwent a curious metamorphosis from being docile, well behaved children, to screaming clamorous demons, giving vent to vociferous appellations, and colorful scurrilities. Finally, they shouted, as a parting gesture, "Go back townies, go back townies," in a repetitious frenzy of conjured up hatred. They pulled at their patched up clothing, and pointed jeeringly at Janie's boots buttoned halfway up the calves of her legs.

Country bumpkins thought Janie to herself. What do they know anyway, stuck away in these small townships all their lives never daring to venture anywhere else. How extremely insulated their lives must be. She did not realize at the time how she would come to love this place and all its residents.

Chapter XXIII

School next day was no better. Janie found herself sitting on a stool in the corner of the classroom with a dunce's hat on her head. The brim was so big it covered her eyes. The crown went a long way up, terminating in a point, resembling a witch's hat. At first she was exceedingly embarrassed, but as the hours wore on, her imagination took flight, and she became the most dreaded witch of all time. Riding on her broomstick, she was chasing the nasty Mr. York, in company with some of the children, into the dense woods around Laindon Hills. Every time he tried to come out of the woods, she would jump down on him, letting out a terrible roar, and he would run back again.

She was brought back to reality again, as she felt herself unceremoniously pushed off the stool she was sitting on. The class was filing out for sports it seemed. She prided herself as a fast runner, and hoped she would be allowed to run in some of the races.

Mr. York approached her. "I have set you some work to do, Janie. I trust that by the time we all get back, you will have completed it to my satisfaction."

"Yes, sir," she replied, feeling very downcast at her exclusion from the sport.

Many times in the course of her work, she would look longingly out of the window at the class, now engaged in their various sports activities. It was a bright sunny day, with just a flicker of a breeze. It would have been good to be out there with the others. Wiping away her tears, she tried hard to apply herself to the task the teacher had set her. She was finding the going hard, as most of the work seemed above her head.

Eventually the class was back again, each one peering with interest at her as they passed. She looked into each face for some gleam of friendship, but there was none. One girl did smile, however. Mr. York called her over. She knew what she was in for, for she had done very little. Once again, she was placed on the stool, this time without the hat. On the way home, she told Milly about her terrible day at school. She was very sympathetic, and promised to help her with her lessons that evening.

Chapter XXIV

Next morning on the way to school, Janie passed the girl who had smiled at her in the classroom the day before. She joined their group, introducing herself as Eileen Davenport. She lived only four doors away; she had wanted to come and say hello when they first moved in but her mother had cautioned her to wait a while. They chatted away as they approached the school. A large crowd had gathered blocking their path. It sounded like a fight taking place. Brenda made it her business to push through to see what she could find out.

"Just what I thought," she said, "It's Michael Dunn at it again." She shouted at him, "You bully, pick on someone your own size Michael Dunn." He left off beating the small boy and came after her, "Take that." He pushed a clenched fist into her back. She rounded on him.

"That's right, hit girls, more your mark." He made as though to make another lunge at her, but the others stood around to protect her. "One day," she was heard to say, "he will meet his match." The bell rang and the crowd dispersed.

Chapter XXV

Mrs. Upjohn, who so far, had not had any dealings with the newly arrived family, was at present watching from a window. Bill was busy tackling the weeds and digging the back garden. She thought she liked the look of him. Indeed, he was an industrious individual, for her husband had noticed him painting the kitchen at two o'clock in the morning after returning from a late council meeting. At this moment, he paused to roll and light a cigarette. He was drawing on the lighted cigarette, when his eyes, which had been restlessly traversing the garden, came to rest on what was evidently a small pile of wood. Going across, he began to examine it. There were several useful pieces he discovered, which could be set aside for the building of the fowl house he had in mind. Colonel Upjohn came out into the garden.

"I'll say, old chap." Bill turned round towards where the voice was coming from.

"I may as well introduce myself. I'm Upjohn, Colonel Upjohn. And you're Reynolds, aren't you? Or so I was informed." The two men shook hands.

"Thinking of building a chicken shed?" Bill nodded. "You'll find some more wood lying about in the fields."

"Ha, yes, right ho." Bill got tied up with his h's when faced with a man of some education. The Colonel was speaking again,

"A lot of hard work ahead of you, but it's certainly the right time of the year to put plants and seeds in, eh what."

"Ha, that's for sure," replied Bill. Silence fell between them. The Colonel broke it.

"Well, old chap, mustn't detain a good man from his work. Goodbye for now." Calling his dog, he walked up the pathway that separated his immaculate flower garden from his immaculate vegetable garden. Bill's eyes ran enviously over them. He couldn't wait to get cracking on his own garden, for he was anxious for the produce to enable his family to make ends meet. He turned his attention to the wood. Before long he was able to make some sort of a start on the chicken house, watched in secret by the Upjohns, who themselves had very little to do. Children had never been born to them, there was nobody to untidy their house or garden.

Chapter XXVI

Another week had passed. Bill was not in the garden that weekend, as he was working the alternate shift at the gasworks. The Colonel, feeling a sense of loss, as he began to like seeing him around, took the trouble to ask Victoria where he was.

"He's working this weekend," she informed him.

"Ha Mrs. Reynolds, I'm sorry to hear that. He always looks such a mess coming from that place. Couldn't he get a job closer to home?" There was a short silence. "Perhaps I could do something," said the Colonel. He continued, "I notice your husband is handy, could he fix a new basin in my bathroom?"

"He could. I'll speak to him when he comes back," said Victoria.

So it came about that Bill carried out the work, but refused payment. The Colonel was able to obtain enough wood to enable him to complete his chicken shed. Mrs. Upjohn began to speak more freely with them, and would often be seen speaking to Janie, whom she grew to be quite fond of.

Chapter XXVII

Eileen Davenport was coming down the garden path. She had come to fetch Janie, whom she had invited to tea. Four houses up may have been a comparatively short distance in Plinters Street, but in country areas, these were often multiplied, due to the fact that the amount of land surrounding an individual house could sometimes be several acres, so it was a fair walk to Eileen's house. The back door opened straight into the dining room and it was filled with children, four older than Eileen and three younger. Her mother entered the room as they both arrived carrying large bowls of food. She was a rather tall woman, having dark curly hair set against a skin that had a perennial tan. A close look would reveal many lines around the eyes, caused no doubt by screwing them up in the sunshine of many a summer. She went to the back door and called her husband in for dinner.

Janie noticed he was a stockily built man, and very short; in fact, she was actually taller than him. He also had a club foot. He stared hard at her when she was introduced, his eyes, it seemed were making mental calculations. She must have passed the test, for the next moment he was smiling, he asked her to sit down and make herself at home. For all their poverty, the family assembled round the large old table and seemed, to Janie, to exude an aura of love and well being. It was certainly an enviable home environment, despite their so obviously lack of material assets.

The family, like so many others at this time, was very poor. Alas, they were too proud to accept charity, or any offers of help from outsiders. They preferred to keep such people away from their door. Janie was asked which part of London she came from. Only Mr. Davenport appeared to know London, the rest of the family had never been there. They all spoke of it as if it was a different country. In consequence, she found herself the focal point of their attention, and what is more, she liked it.

Too soon, it was time to go home. Janie thanked them for providing such a nice meal, saying the chicken and veggies were lovely. They all, much to Janie's surprise, laughed at this. What delightful ignorance, they must have been thinking.

"Janie! That was a rabbit, commonly known as 'poor man's chicken'. Have you never tasted it before? We go out trapping them," said Mr. Davenport.

"Yes, poor man's chicken Janie," added John, confirming what his father had said. John was the eldest son. It was now quite dark, Burt (Mr. Davenport), offered to see her home. Janie gladly accepted.

On the way, they were met by Bill, who had been watching out for her. The two men peered at each other in the twilight and shook hands affably. After a pause, Bert extended an invitation to Bill and his family, to meet at his house on the following Monday. His invitation was gladly accepted.

Chapter XXVIII

The past few days had turned out very warm considering it was still only spring and according to the B.B.C. Weather forecast, it was likely to remain so for the rest of the weekend. After an early breakfast for the Reynolds that Saturday morning, the task allotted to the children was to heap up all the rubbish found in the long grass. Bill was set to dig for most of the day. Both girls stopped at the chicken shed to peer in at the newly acquired brown hen, as she now lay on her eggs. Katie was a very tame old bird, an old brooder with a long history of hatching, so Bill was informed when he had acquired her at the local auctions. Any day now, they learned, the eggs would hatch. Ted, also was taking a great deal of interest, and inquired of the girls if they had hatched yet. He seemed disappointed on learning the answer was no.

Numerous items of interest were found amongst the grass including daffodils and narcissi. The girls began picking them to take inside. The sounds of voices, hailing Ted and George, made them both turn round. They were met with Uncle Dan and Aunties Rose and May, together with five cousins from Plinters Street. Everyone immediately went inside the house. Altogether, the work was, for the time being, forgotten. Barely had the tea finished brewing, when the multitudinous ringing of bicycle bells filled the air, bringing everyone out to the front again. Five brothers and a younger sister of Grace and Victoria, with four of their friends, had ridden all the way from London to spend the weekend with them.

"We've brought our tents," they were heard to say. Bill said that they were welcome to sleep anywhere they liked inside or outside. After a light snack, the men went out with Bill to take a look around. Colonel Upjohn could be seen talking to some of them, and before very long he was passing over his garden tools for the general use of the company, as he so blithely put it.

Uncle Charlie, who was one of the visitors, had lived with the Reynolds for two years when he was younger, so the girls knew him very well, compared with their other uncles. He offered to dig a patch of ground for them to sow seeds. They crowded round him eagerly asking, as he was digging, for worms to feed Katie, the brown hen. When he had broken up all the lumps and had raked the soil to a fine tilth, he put his hands into his pockets, and brought out some money.

"Here, a penny for each of you to spend." He handed a shilling over to Milly saying, "Buy some flower and vegetable seeds with that – off you go!"

Thanking him, they ran to Bamford's Store, taking Ted and George with them. By the time they returned, he already had furrowed out the shallow drill in the soil to take the seeds. He opened up the seed packets, and taking the radish seeds, he first of all emptied some of these into each packet. At their puzzled looks, he laughed, saying, "Radishes are the first to germinate, so you can see just where the seed rows are. By the time the others come through, the radishes will be ready to eat."

"Yuk, I hate radishes," said Brenda.

Grace and Max arrived for Brenda and Egan, but on seeing most of the family had turned up, they decided to stay for the rest of the day. The women prepared the food while the men worked in the garden. Soon, May called them all in for dinner.

After having dined, Ernest and Alf suggested they all cycle into the village to buy some plants. This suggestion was taken up by the rest, and they decided to pool money for the purpose. Bert Davenport arrived at the open back door. "Would any of you care for a walk down to the club? It's open at seven this evening and families and friends are always made welcome." They all agreed to finish the garden by six that evening.

Victoria put one of her famous bread puddings in the oven, ensuring that the coal range was kept down at a low temperature. "It will be cooked by eleven tonight," she said. Nothing was wasted as far as food was concerned, even the stale bread was used. It was soaked in cold water for an hour or more, then all the water was squeezed out of the bread and then placed into a bowl with knobs of butter, sultanas, mixed spices, black molasses and dark treacle. It was then placed in deep tin – more spices were then sprinkled and knobs of butter put on top. It was baked in a low coal oven for 4 hours. When coming in from the cold, the smell of hot bread pudding made your tummy rumble.

The children asked if they could play the gramophone on the patio. After changing the needle and winding the handle, they turned the trumpet into the direction of the wind. They found a record they could waltz to, and were soon dancing on the patio. Uncle George stopped working to watch them, but it was not long before he could resist the temptation to join in himself. He began by admonishing them as to the correct ways of ballroom dancing. He invited one of the women to dance with him, in order that he could demonstrate. Everyone was keen to join in and learn, for Uncle George was famed for his prowess on the dance floor. He was also a well known professional dancer. So for the rest of the afternoon until tea was announced, they all took lessons in dancing.

The Davenport family arrived on time, to find them all still in the throes of preparation. Lizzie began to count the children assembled there. "There's eighteen altogether, and I can count nineteen adults, including myself." Uncle Charlie and his friends had arrived back pushing their cycles up the garden path. They sat Ted, on a cushion on one of the cycles, and George was placed on a seat at the back of another. Bert told Victoria he had arranged for herself and Mrs. Davenport and most of the young children, to be brought back in a car owned by a member of the club, who was also a good friend of his.

There was very little traffic on the lane along which they were walking, and they were thereby able to spread out, taking their time and talking. Altogether, thought Janie, they were a happy bunch of people, whose happiness she enjoyed sharing.

It was a beautiful late spring evening, with the sounds of glorious bird song; leaves of the trees were tinged with gold in the rays of the setting sun. The air smelt fresh and sweet, in keeping with the fecundity of the season. One could feel the sap rising in one's very being. From the many farmyards came the sounds of crackling wood, which, combined with smoke, twirled high, and floated quickly away on the breeze.

After dinner tomorrow (Max was speaking in one of his rare outbursts) we could all take a walk to the hills, it's a beautiful view from the top. Grace, who grew excited at this suggestion, interrupted saying, "We could go picking wild flowers in the woods." John Davenport began to speak of the lovely old Gothic church. "I know the one you mean," said Grace.

"Bit spooky to my way of thinking!" I don't much care for all those spouting gargoyles, I think you call them." Daisy spoke of a quaint hotel on the hill top. They could have afternoon tea there of course.

"What a smashing idea," said Doris. She was the youngest sister, in Victoria's family.

They eventually turned into the cinder track, hemmed in by the woods on the right side and the railway on the other. As they passed the railway station, Uncle Dave, ran in to inquire the times of the trains back to London on Sunday evening.

The club, when they arrived there, proved to be quite a large hall. A placard placed on the counter told everyone that members' fees were five shillings per annum. Visitors accompanied by members, had to pay sixpence. Inside were numerous tables with chairs placed round the walls. A large stage at the back was set out in drums, piano and other musical instruments. Drinks could be had at the bar. The children were bought crisps and soft drinks. After about half an hour, a voice came over the microphone, "Can anyone play a musical instrument, as our players will not be turning up this evening." There was an immediate response as Bert offered to play the trumpet, Bill the drums and Victoria the piano. Somebody else from the crowd offered to play the concertina. Also a talent quest for the adults was got under way. There was also one for the children. When the band struck up, adults and children were soon dancing. The evening turned out a big success, everyone claimed they had enjoyed themselves.

Walking back after the social, they held a sing song, and sang many songs in currency at the time, as well as some of the past. As they came within a short distance of 'Bognor Regis' their nostrils were assailed by the smell of Victoria's large bread pudding still cooking in the oven. "Smells good," Bert was heard to remark. "Let's have a game of cards," suggested Bill. They all trooped down the garden path to the house. Janie, who lingered behind to savor the remains of the day's happiness, looked at the billions of stars twinkling in the sky, recalling that day in the past, when her beautiful dress had been ruined. The stars, she thought tonight, were really on her side.

Chapter XXIX

"Janie, have you, by chance, eaten the rest of the condensed milk? I haven't any left in the pantry to make your dad's tea batch."

"I haven't had it mum, honest, I haven't," said Janie. "I'll go round to Auntie Grace's if you like mum, she usually has some spare milk."

"But it's nearly midnight, and pitch black outside. Milly is asleep, it's not fair to go waking her up."

"Can't I take Rose with me? I'll feel quite safe in her company," pleaded Janie. During the conversation between the two, Rose had been looking from one to the other, as if waiting for the happy outcome. After all, like most dogs, she was always ready for a stroll, no matter what hour. At the sound of her name, she wagged her tail in happy anticipation.

"I wouldn't normally consider this Janie, but I suppose, as your dad has to leave at four in the morning, I haven't much choice in the matter."

"Don't worry mum, I'll run very fast."

Rose followed close to her heels as they made their way in the darkness. The night always held a fascination for Janie; its world seemed so far removed from day with its all too familiar realities, like school and games and being chided by mum for eating the milk. Out here in the dark, there was mystery. She had the feeling that she was one with the universe. She could descry the firmament as she looked up at the sky between the tall trees. She could hear the owls hooting from their invisible recesses in the forest, and the incessant chirping of the crickets. A large bat swooped down close to her. She felt a movement of air round her face where it had skimmed very close. She raised her hand as if to prevent any getting tangled in her hair. The thought of that happening horrified her. As she came out into the opening away from the trees, she noticed a ditch on one side of the lane in which were embedded hundreds of glowworms, shining like miniature stars, she thought.

There was no moon tonight and it was very dark. Rose suddenly darted ahead, but came back again as Janie softly chided her. She and Rose were close companions. The well read Uncle Max would often pull her leg about this misquoting Kipling in the phrase, "And never the twain shall part."

They now turned from the lane which again entered the forest, leading to Aunt Grace's cottage. Red glowing eyes appeared and then disappeared. Rose suddenly barked, eager to give chase to the rabbits. The silence was broken again by a dog howling in the distance. On entering the garden, she was glad to see by the lights, just discernible behind the curtain, that the occupants were still up. She knocked. Aunt Grace's voice reached her from the opened window, "Who is it?"

"It's me, Janie."

"My goodness, whatever are you doing out at this time of the night child? Is there anything wrong?"

"No, it's alright Auntie. I've come for some milk. Mum is out of it, and she wants some for dad, who has to be away early in the morning." She handed Janie a tin of milk.
"Now you must hurry home as fast as you can darling. Ah! You have Rose with you, that's good."

On the way back, the sounds of a motorcycle approaching came to their ears. She hugged Rose to her, but felt the hairs on the dog's back stand up as she listened intently. They stood in the shelter of a bush until it passed them, then they made a dash for home.

Victoria was very relieved to see her back again. Janie was high in her praises for Rose, who was turning out to be an excellent house dog and companion for the children. They had the feeling she could understand every word uttered.

"Tie Rose up for the night, will you Janie. I hope she doesn't slip her chain again. I believe your dad said he'll be buying a stronger chain for her." Janie looked at Rose and could not help noticing she had indeed the small size of a Pomeranian, but the strong wiry framework of a chow.

Chapter XXX

The rain seemed to fall from a cloudless sky, and went as suddenly as it came, lending a bright clean freshness to everything. The ditches on either side of the road had filled up fast, as water poured into them from surrounding hills. Stepping from the shelter of a tree, Janie continued her walk home. Ahead of her walked a young woman pushing a very high pram. A large plum duff dog trotted quietly beside her. She stopped outside the store, applied the pram breaks and muttering a few commands to the dog, walked over to the shop. He lay down beside the pram, and looked after the woman, as she entered the shop.

Suddenly, the pram began to slide down the muddy embankment towards the flooded ditch. Janie, aware of the peril of the situation, began to run forward, realising the baby could be tipped into the ditch if the pram should run askew. Although a very fast runner, she did not think she could make it in time. The back wheels were now high in the air, and the pram was only inches away from the ditch.

The Dalmatian's leap was awe-inspiring. Its large body seemed to fly through the air. Landing on its back legs, it succeeded in hooking front paws round the handle of the pram. Quivering and slipping in its precarious position, it held on, taking the strain on its back legs, gradually bringing the pram back into the lane, and then laying its body between the pram and the ditch. Amazed at what she had just witnessed, Janie went over to the pram and peered into to see how the baby was faring. She noticed how young the baby looked, no more than about six weeks at the most, she thought. A growl from the dog reminded her that her presence was not welcome.

Coming out of the shop, the woman placed the items in the pram basket, and began to walk back down the lane, oblivious of the drama that had taken place in her absence. The dog, large and ungainly, ambled beside her. Janie was moved by the incident, turning over in her mind, the fact that many such acts of heroism must go unnoticed.

Chapter XXXI

Rose came bounding round the corner of the bungalow to greet her, wagging her ridiculously large tail from side to side, which somehow took her hind legs with it, giving her the appearance of affecting a kind of uncoordinated jig, before she could move forward again. Catching her as she jumped, Janie lost her balance on the wet grass and the two of them tumbled over and over, causing a commotion of barks and laughter. Dogs from other distant gardens excitedly barked their approval, regardless of reprimands from their owners.

Rushing to beat Rose to the house, she slipped on the mat at the entrance, and went sliding under the kitchen table where she lay, helpless with laughter, Rose went skidding past her, crashing against the gleaming brass fender in front of the kitchen range, her long black tongue dripping saliva, as she lay panting for breath. They both looked quietly round at the mess they had made, and the possibility of Victoria turning up at any moment.

The coke had lost its glow in the fire grate, the bread which had been left to bake in the oven smelt as if it was done. Getting up off the floor, Janie found a cloth and opened up the oven door from which she removed, one at a time, four tins of bread, simultaneously tapping them on top for the hollow sound, as she had seen her mother do so many times. She then tipped the bread out of the tins on to the wire rack above the stove. The smell of the freshly baked bread reminded her how hungry she was and she began eagerly to set the table for tea. Having completed this task, she lay down on Teds' couch and in spite of all efforts to stay awake, she fell fast asleep, only vaguely aware that Rose had joined her and lay across her feet.

Chapter XXXII

Janie woke. Rose jumped down and stretched her legs, asking with her eyes to be let out. Janie opened the door. Soon Milly made her appearance, greeting her almost half-heartedly. "Why is the house so quiet? Where is everybody?"

"Don't you remember," said Janie. "Mum has gone to Southend to visit a dentist." At that very moment, Victoria was recovering from the dose of nitrous oxide, which had been given to her prior to having all her top teeth extracted. She was laughing and talking about various family incidents which came to mind. The dentist was saying, "Alright Mrs. Reynolds, you're doing very nicely. I've had to remove all your top teeth. Next week I will have to remove your bottom teeth. Unfortunately, you have pyorrhoea of the gums."

She looked a sorry sight when later she entered the house and they were gathered round the kitchen table. Mr. Davenport, who was now a very close friend of the family, had brought home Ted and George and had assisted in organizing the tea table. It came as a shock to learn that she would have to wear false teeth. Ted thought her very brave having so many teeth removed at once.

"How can you stand wearing false teeth mum?" asked Ted.

"I have to, I've no choice," lisped Victoria. Janie thought back to the time, when not so long ago, her father had to extract his own tooth. He was out of work at the time, and there was barely any food in the house. There was no money to be found to pay a dentist, so he had undertaken some very painful do-it-yourself surgery, which entailed fixing some string between the affected tooth, and the knob of a door, which had to be slammed shut at the appropriate moment. After a number of unsuccessful and painful attempts, the offending tooth was finally extracted, with much bloodshed. This thought had the effect of making her mother's present ordeal less painful to Janie's mind.

Chapter XXXIII

The old thirteenth century church stood on the highest hill overlooking the country. Once it must have been surrounded by dense woods. Now it was separated from them by a narrow road, which undulated in green mounds, carpeted in countless buttercups and daisies. Green and yellow fungi covered the walls; cobwebs hung heavy in layers, embedded with dust and shells of insects, long ago ensnared and now desiccated. Dust also covered the colored windows protected by thick iron bars. It seemed to guard some ghostly secret within its dark confines. The massive heavy iron doors barred all intruders, assisted by the faces, weird and fantastic, molded out of iron, which surrounded the graveyard. It smelt of dampness and decay. The children, after becoming bewilderedly hypnotized and fixed in time, as it were, suddenly took to their heels and ran, thinking, that if they were to stay there any longer, they would soon be snatched from the giant hand of death.

Once safely back on the road, they stopped to look back, feeling safe and glad to be free and alive in the warm sunshine. "Let's pick some bluebells," one of them suggested. Willingly they all agreed, and were soon walking about in large shimmering beds of bluebells, whose colors ranged from very dark blue in the denser parts of the forest, to a very light shade of blue in the open parts.

"I'll gather the Oxford colors, and you can gather the Cambridge colors," said Brenda, who had in mind the boat race, which was due to be held next Saturday. Brenda began to penetrate deeper into the forest, in spite of protests from the others.

"Come back Brenda, don't go alone," said Milly, calling her back. But she went and finally disappeared altogether.

"The fields were full of wild primroses, pansies and violets. Let's look for them," suggested Lizzie. They continued picking flowers in silence, which allowed only the calls of birds and insects. The time came when a black stickiness on their fingers from the sap of the flowers made them reluctant to continue picking.

"I've had enough anyway," said Milly. Brenda had still not joined them. Milly gathered the children together, making sure that there was nobody else missing. They began to grow anxious about Brenda.

"Let's look for her," suggested John. "She could be lost for a long time in these woods." They began shouting her name. After about half an hour of searching, they became alarmed.
"We had better get help." Egan's suggestion was taken up and they all began to move out of the woods.

They took the path which went through the fields, climbing over many styles, on the way home. They forgot Brenda for a short while, as they began to talk among themselves. Janie, was asking Milly why it was possible to walk round, and over fields. This engrossed Milly for a while. She was always ready and eager to expound her knowledge on many subjects. She was sometimes nicknamed the 'walking encyclopedia'.

"It's an old English custom," she explained, "that if you carry a corpse over a field, you immediately establish a right of way. It's only what I've read of course, so whether it's true or false, I couldn't tell you Janie." One of the younger children lost a shoe. Eileen volunteered to go back and retrieve it, and as she did so, she happened to spot Brenda darting between two trees. She was following up, but remaining concealed. She told the others who became very angry at Brenda's subterfuge.

"That's mean of her. We've left our flowers behind because of her. Let's go to the swings, and we won't speak to her when she arrives." Janie, on hearing their plans, immediately ran ahead, for she wanted the high-seated swing. To take the short cut, she would have to pass the cattle. The others would go the long way, she thought. She emerged on the highest part of the slope leading down to the swings situated in the corner of the paddock. She stopped in her tracks. A strange sight had met her eyes. What appeared to be an illuminated round house had blocked her path. Putting her hand to her eyes to shield them from the dazzling brightness of the dome like roof, she stood petrified and frightened. Right before Janie's eyes stood three men in suits of strange design. Hoods covered their heads a clear band of translucent substance about their eyes apparently enabled them to see. Catching sight of Janie, one beckoned her over. Fear rooted her to the spot; hadn't Mother always said, "Never go with strange men." The one who had waved now walked over to her. She wanted to run away, but her legs felt too heavy to lift. He seemed very kind, for he took her hand as if expecting her, and they walked together towards the entrance.

As she entered the strange interior, it at first seemed dark, just like the church, she used to visit when she lived in London. A very strange effect occurred as she moved inside. It seemed to expand, and what was more, she had the feeling that this could go on indefinitely. There seemed to be rows upon rows of blinking lights everywhere, imparting a preternatural glow to the seemingly dark interior. Her hand, still held by one of the strangers, was pressed reassuringly. He took her into what appeared to be another chamber, stranger, in appearance than the last one. There was a round white table in the center. Something large lay in the middle of it. A huge clear circular shaped object descended from above and covered it. Janie watched with fascination, as a shaft of light appeared from which source, she could not tell, as it began to hover over everything. It moved from the object on the table to focus on the man at her side. He held up a hand and it moved away out of sight. Another man entered the room. Both looked at each other and then at her. A small part of the floor rose up and opened into a seat. She was placed in it and slowly it began turning round. The man holding her hand then removed his hood. She had seen his face before it was the priest in the church who had made the sign of the cross over her? Her chair now faced a huge screen which showed her the 'pyramids' Janie remembered, and still does the narrow passageway she climbed. There was a small opening in one wall, she squeezed her way through and stepped into what was a small room, and following his instructions, she retrieved what seemed like small scrolls of stiff paper. She could smell the musty air as fear filled her heart. Opening one of the scrolls, she saw what looked like complex symbols. The unusual stranger conveyed to Janie that these symbols represented complicated mathematics that would one day help mankind explore space and visit other worlds. Why was she, only a child at the time, shown these scrolls? Janie was to ponder these thoughts a lot later in life.

Janie found herself once more in the blinding light of day. The children were shouting as they came running down the embankment to pick out their favorite swing. "Come on Janie," Eileen was calling, "Let's see who can swing the highest." Janie was still far away, but looking at what appeared to be a black round circle on the grass. She wanted so much to tell them what had happened to her, but she knew that they would only laugh, disbelievingly. That evening she confided in her mother what had happened to her, only to be severely scolded for talking such nonsense and she was never to speak of these sorts of thing to other people. So Janie remained silenced on the matter for many years

Chapter XXXIV

The table had been laid the night before, a custom the Reynolds continued from their days in London. Bill made the tea, it being Sunday. This was also another family custom. While it was brewing, he put the Sunday special on each saucer, two custard cream biscuits. On Janie's saucer, he placed three – two for her and one for Rose, the dog. She would be in the bedroom waiting for it. He looked into the tin for milk, it was empty. He was certain it had been full last evening. Going to the pantry he opened up another tin.

"Wakie, wakie; tea up!" He called as he reached the bedrooms. Rubbing the sleep out of their eyes, both girls sat up in bed, pleased that dad was able to have Sundays off from work it was good having him home, after seeing so little of him during the week. Today was also the first of May. He looked at Janie sternly, "Now look here young lady, you've been at the tinned milk again, haven't you? Now I want the truth."

"Yes dad, but I didn't think you'd notice, because I only had two teaspoonfuls, honestly dad."
"I would say a whole tin full would be more like it, my lady. It has got to stop. I'm on the early morning shift next week, and woe betide you if I'm left without milk to make up me tea batches." Janie nodded her head in evident contrition,

yet not able to understand why a whole tin full should disappear. Somebody else, she thought must be tucking into the milk.

Rose sat and begged for her biscuit and Janie gave it to her. After they had finished drinking their tea, Rose took their cups away. She picked them up by the handles with her teeth, carried them to the kitchen, and standing upright on her hind legs, placed them carefully on the table. The boys shouted out to Rose to come and collect their cups also. The girls got up straight away to bathe. This, being a special day, Victoria had laid out the dresses she had made for the occasion.

Milly brushed her hair; it had darkened and was now brown in color. Victoria had curled Janie's hair round a dolly peg and as she pulled it out, long curls were seen to fall over her shoulders. They then donned their white dresses, which were trimmed with frills of red, white and blue, matching the ribbons in their hair. Other members of the family wore their best attire. All then trooped out to join other families on their way to the village green. Colonel Upjohn offered to give Ted and George a lift in his car, and to look after them until the family arrived.

It was May-Day, the first of May, and it was custom to all meet on the village green and for the children to dance around the maypoles in celebration. The maypoles stood apart from each other in a large circle. Red, white and blue streamers fell from a circle of steel, situated at the top of each pole. The boys dressed in blue trousers, white shirts and red ties, had the appearance of having been given a thorough scrubbing by their mothers before coming out. The girls, after having to wait, found the time and the inclination to eye each other's dresses. They all now took up their places. A girl stood beside each boy. The music struck up as each one stepped forward to take a braid. They then began weaving under the outstretched arms of one child, then around the next one, until the braid had been woven into a pattern on each pole. The onlookers clapped with admiration.

Very soon, tea and refreshments were being handed round, and the atmosphere of jollity was seen to transmit to old and young alike. The parson was seen to mix with his parishioners. The council members present were taking advantage of the situation to impress their personalities on the rich and influential present.

By four o'clock the last of the families had left for home. Daisy Davenport was heard to say that this had been the best May Day festivity she had known for a long time. Bert winked shyly at the others, "She says this every year without fail, all the same though, it was kind of special this year, I will admit."

On reaching home, Bill went immediately to bed, as he had to rise early next morning. The rest of the family sat round the kitchen table engaging themselves in making a large rag mat. We used to cut up old coats and garments into small even pieces and then we would get a wool hook plus a canvas and twist the rag pieces around the hook, run it through the canvas and knot them. As the evening wore on, Victoria lit the lamp. It was a lovely clear night, the girls went outside, and were soon looking up at the stars. Janie always wondered about the universe, its purpose and extent. She had been informed in books that she had read that the sun around which they circled was only a very mediocre star. Situated in turn at the edge of one of the millions of galaxies, said to be speeding through the Universe – whatever that was – at so many thousands of miles a second. Poor Milly was subjected to the usual bombardment of questions, which of course she did her best to answer as the occasion demanded. They were interrupted by Victoria, calling them in for bed.

Chapter XXXV

Bill was home when the girls arrived from school. He was unusually quiet at the dinner table that evening. After the meal he called Janie to him.

"Janie, I warned you yesterday about the milk disappearing. We can't afford to keep buying the stuff just because you can't leave it alone. If you want milk, why there's plenty of goat's milk you can have to drink."

"But dad, I didn't touch the milk last night, honestly I didn't."
"You were last to bed Janie, I was listening."
"Yes, I was," admitted Janie.
"Then for Christ's sake, who else would have it?"
"Not me, dad, honest," wailed poor Janie.
"Come Janie, the truth."

"Oh, but I didn't dad, I'm speaking the truth." Her eyes were on his hands, as he began unbuckling his belt.

"I'm afraid I'll have to strap you my girl, if only for your lies." Before long she was feeling the strap, as it wrapped itself around her legs. The psychological pain of not being believed, she felt, far outweighed her physical pain. She broke down and cried. Rose ran under the table and Milly and Ted went to their room.

"Well, Janie, what have you to say now?"
"I didn't do it," gasped Janie. She ran out the room and threw herself on her bed. Rose came in and licked her hands. Janie cuddled her round the neck.

The alarm clock went off at four o'clock. Jack felt for the torch, and made his way to the kitchen. He saw what he thought was a large object on the table. He shone his torch on it. It was Rose. She made a dash for the door, but he quickly closed it. Lighting the lamp, he looked on the table and saw the empty milk tin – sparkling clean. He was amazed that the dog could lick it so clean. He should have gathered from this on past occasions, that this should not have pointed to Janie. Why would she want to clean the tin up after her? Poor kid, he would have to make amends to her over this. But he would face that problem tonight. He called the dog to him, she ran under the table. He bent under the table to wrest her out, but she immediately darted behind the couch. All right, my girl, I'll deal with you when I return tonight, just you wait.

Chapter XXXVI

Rose ran to meet the children from school and dashed excitedly around their legs as they walked home. As they neared home, their nostrils were assailed by the smell of cakes cooking in the oven. Cousins and friends turned in at the gate to investigate what their mother had been making. On the rack over the range stood a plate piled high with what looked like delicious doughnuts. There were more sizzling away in the hot fat underneath. There was no sign of either Victoria or Grace.

They were informed by Ted that they had gone to the local store. The children waited a short while.

"They must be talking to Mrs. Bamford, let's take one, I'm starving," Milly said. She took one and the rest followed suit. They ran out onto the patio, where they put their teeth hungrily into the golden cookies. But their teeth stuck fast. They desperately pulled at the doughnuts in their mouths only to find that they stretched into a sticky, gluey rope and their jaws were clamped tightly together. Frantically, they tried to communicate, one with the other, by means of signs. But looking so funny, each to the other, they all broke into uncontrolled giggling. The sound came out of their noses, blocking their ears. Ted, who was laughing at them from the open window, shouted, "Serves you right for pinching them." They shook their fists at him. When Grace and Victoria rounded the corner of the bungalow, they were first of all nonplussed, but on recovering and gaining and inkling of what they must have done, both broke down with laughter.

"Isn't it so much quieter without all their yapping," said Victoria. "Shall we leave them to it?" Grace replied.

"What do you think we did wrong?" asked Grace. The children tried to beckon for help.
"It will have to be soap and water to wash it away." They shook their heads.

"Well, it's up to you." There followed a very reluctant procession to the wash house, where some time was to be spent in removing the offending mixture.

Chapter XXXVII

Bill entered the door, glad to be home again, after his usual hard day's work. Rose ran to meet him, but changed her mind, and ran under the table instead. "What's wrong girl?" Ted called to her.

"She knows," Bill replied. As he picked up the empty milk tin from where he had put it that morning, she made a bolt for the door. But it was shut. Taking off his belt, he began laying it round her. She growled in defiance, baring her teeth at him.

"You're in the wrong my girl, and you know it," said Bill. She yelped in pain. Janie entered to see what was going on. Rose ran to her. Janie cuddled her looking hard at her father.

"I'm very sorry Janie, about yesterday, I mean. I never thought Rose would have done it." Janie tossed her curls at him and she and Rose left the room.

But a few days later, she relented. She gave her father a kiss and decided the misunderstanding should be forgotten. "How about you Rose?" he asked. She got up and reversed her position on the floor, her backside facing towards him. Her ears pricked up at the sound of his voice and her tail gave a few thumps on the floor, but she continued facing away, much to the amusement of everyone. But it was not long before her doggie heart relented. Certainly, from that day onwards, no further infiltrations were made on the tins of condensed milk.

Chapter XXXVIII

Poor Sidney from the start he never stood a chance. He stood at the gate watching as they performed acrobats on the front lawn. He managed to catch Millya eye.

"Do the Reynolds live here? I'm Sid, your mum's youngest brother."
"Come with us, mum will be pleased to see you." replied Milly - and she was.

"The same age as Milly and Brenda, only half a head taller. I think, you could do with filling out a bit. Are you hungry? How long can you stay?" Victoria asked.

They were surprised by his ignorance of the most elementary of things. He didn't even know what a cow looked like.

"He's dumb," Brenda said. "Let's play games on him." In the days that followed, he'd be heard to say, "I'm sorry I came."

"Townee! Townee!" they would sing as he sulked his way home. They would become genuinely contrite of their treatment of him, all except Brenda. The next day he followed them, feeling very fed up and saying, "I'll go back to London tomorrow. I'm sorry I came for my holidays here." Brenda was quick to detect tears in his eyes -"Cry-baby!"
"I'm not," he declared hotly, "You're just a horrible girl and I hate you." The rest of the children were as good as their word, to make his last few days happy ones. Victoria had tea ready when they got home.

"I know it's rather early to eat, but I've taken a job cooking the evening meal for a family, until the regular woman gets back from her holidays. With Milly off to high school soon, we shall need that extra money. I should like you all to tuck in and look after Ted and George while I'm gone." They all assured her that she need not worry, as everything would be taken care of.

All went well during the evening until they thought they heard cries of a kitten. The family had recently acquired one. A search began, and it was traced to the roof of the outside lavatory. It was some distance above ground level and therefore difficult to reach, and no attempts at standing on a chair could reach it. They decided to wait until dad got home. He had locked the ladder in the shed and had the key in his pocket. However, the cries from the kitten were getting them down. They urged Sid to try by some means to rescue the little animal. Very reluctantly, he managed to haul himself up on to the new asbestos roof. The roof caved in and he very promptly disappeared. On opening the door, they were horrified to see him immersed, head and shoulders in the nearly full bucket lavatory, which the night man was due to empty that night. His body and legs were up right, they managed to pull him free. At first, their instinct was to run from him, because of the terrible smell that came from him. It was so overpowering in fact, that they turned the hose on him, which did not meet with his approval, seeing that it was ice cold well water! The final touch of irony came, when the kitten appeared, unharmed, having finally jumped off the roof in fright.

When the situation had improved, and Sid was thoroughly cleaned down, the realization of what had happened dawned on them. The lavatory roof had only been installed a week ago, in place of the old one. It was decided that they should all go to bed early and pretend to be asleep, for they knew it would not be long before either parent would be back. Perhaps, in the morning, dad might not mind so much if his discovery of the disaster could be postponed!

It was eight o'clock when Victoria and Bill met at the gate. Prior to entering the house, Bill's first words were, "It's very quiet. In fact, it's a bit too quiet. Something has happened, I'll bet my bottom dollar on it."

"I'll check the rooms," said Victoria. At the sound of their footsteps in the house, the children feigned to be asleep. She looked in on them.

"They're asleep," she assured Bill. He shook his head.

" They've been up to something. I'll be bound." He began to search every room while the children held their breath. "I dunno," he said, sitting down at last to his meal, "There's something wrong and I'm going to find out, if it takes me all night."

Victoria knew that once her husband was possessed of a hunch, she could not shake him out of it. He always had the uncanny knack of knowing about things, as the saying went.

Eventually, things began to settle down. As conversation had stopped altogether, the children guessed that their father must have dropped off to sleep in the armchair, as was his custom, before retiring to bed. They also heard the clicking of knitting needles, where Victoria had commenced to knit.

"Dad's gone to sleep," they whispered hopefully to each other, as his faint snores became perceptible to them through the walls. "Perhaps by tomorrow he'll not feel so bad when he discovers it." It was a forlorn hope which they were willing to nurse.

It was eleven o'clock when Jack woke up and yawned. "Time for bed," he was heard to say. The children, still awake, were relieved to hear this, as very soon he was pushing the back door bolt into place. A few minutes later, however, he changed his mind, unbolted the back door, and made his way to the toilet. He had not been sitting on the seat for a full minute, when he became aware of a strong draft of air making him feel uncomfortable. He began to look around, starting with the floor, his gaze gradually moved upwards. As he raised his eyes to the roof, he became aware that the stars were winking brightly down at him. His new roof, what had happened to it? Then the penny dropped. All was clear to him at last. "I knew it, the buggers!" Almost falling over his trousers, he quickly made his way into the house, making a beeline for the children's bedrooms.

"Alright the lot of you, you don't need to pretend you're asleep. I'll deal with you all in the morning." In fact, it was a long time before anyone could sleep that night.

Sleep hadn't mellowed their father, as they all hoped it would, for on the following morning he was to tell them in no uncertain manner, that all their treats for the next few months would stop, until there was sufficient money to replace the toilet roof. As for Sid, if it wasn't for the fact that only one day of his holidays remained, he would have been dispatched immediately. Sid, if the truth be known, would have preferred to have been dispatched there and then. They were all sorry and quite prepared to accept their punishment and pleased that they had got off without receiving the belt.

Chapter XXXIX

Where had they come from and where were they all going? No one could cross the main road until the long line of gaudy, but gaily colored hut like caravans had passed. The horses plodded, two by two, their manes and tails plaited with brightly colored braids, and from which hung dozens of tiny brass bells. The latter, were also hanging from around their ears and round their hooves.

They bespoke a tale of travel, excitement, mysticism and magic, which was made more pronounced by their silvery jingle. The occupants, dark skinned, dark eyed and unsmiling, sat on their high seats staring and being stared at.

There were handsome youths with large circular gold earrings in their ears, which set off the beautiful colored scarves round their heads. They were dressed in tight fitting trousers, frilly balloon like blouses and fitted waistcoats of many hues. They handed out, to the watching crowd, crude hand written pamphlets, announcing the arrival of their circus. Their bold eyes would flash deliberately at any pretty miss, who would react by blushing and lowering their eyes.

On reaching the corner, the caravans branched off the road into the track which led to Farmer Harrison's Farm. Unlike most of the farmers around, the latter was of the land – hard working, but helpful towards others. He would often turn a blind eye to a little apple scrumping by the local lads and lassies. "Oy were a boy meself once," was a constant preamble of his. His red apple like face would often crinkle up with laughter, when he related an anecdote of his own now far away childhood. It seemed that the gypsies were aware of his reputation for being easy going and were now prepared to take full advantage of it. Their reputation for thieving and other misdemeanors was a byword wherever they went, and they were not exactly made welcome in Laindon Hills, as time would tell.

Within two days, the women of the tribe, with babies strapped to their backs and carrying a large hand woven cane baskets looped over their arms, were wending their way among the Denizens of the district for the purpose of selling their wares. One was coming up the pathway of "Bognor Regis" causing Rose to bark furiously. On reaching the door, she turned and held the dog in her gaze, causing her to cease barking. Already strange rumors about these people had begun to circulate. The gypsy knocked on the door. As Victoria emerged, the latter's eyes narrowed as her voice came out in a whining singing tone, "Pretty lady buy my wares – scarves, pegs, pins..." As Victoria stepped down to look, the gypsy draped a brightly colored scarf around her neck. "It looks beautiful on you lady, just your color." As she fingered the silk about her neck, Victoria began observing the child on the woman's back. It was grubby and ill dressed. Two girls were standing on the doorstep looking in at Ted. They also displayed squalor and general raggedness and they had nothing on their feet. As she looked a smile crossed the gypsy's face, "You have Bambinos yes?" Victoria nodded. Yes, she too had Bambinos. She pulled her purse out and paid for the scarf. But again the whining tone came at her, "Cross my palm with silver and I will tell the pretty lady's fortune." A crinkled worn hand was already extended in anticipation. Impulsively, Victoria placed a florin into the woman's brown hand. Greedy fingers furled themselves round the coin, which disappeared with alacrity into a large hidden pocket. Looking into her hand, she began, in a different sort of voice, to tell her fortune.

"You're good; a generous lady. Good fortune will come your way. There will be travel to distant lands, but there will be sorrow there. You will live to a very ripe old age. Your husband will die before you, but he will be an old man too. There will be no more children born to you."

The gypsy thanked Victoria, then turned and left. She waited at the gate for the other children to join her. They had found their way into the house and were fingering items on the mantelpiece. Victoria thought she had some shoes that would fit them. She went to the cupboard and brought out two pairs which Bill had only recently mended. A pair of Milly's fitted the older girl. The woman came back again and was very grateful for the shoes, but when she was offered a pair of Janie's for the younger girl, she shrank from touching them. She quickly gathered the children and left again, leaving a very puzzled Victoria looking after her as she finally disappeared from sight. "They'd say anything for money," she thought.

Even Ted was allowed to go with the children to the circus. They took the short cut towards Farmer Harrison's farm. The gypsies had picked the highest spot on which to park their caravans. The horses were grazing in the late lush grass of spring, minus their decorations. A few very large tents were scattered around. There were people standing around them, their attention drawn by the many attractive prizes that could be won. The children were able to go round trying them all.

A woman stood in front of a large tent, wearing a thick jersey, riding boots and breeches. She was holding a whip in her hand. A man was holding forth on her prowess and great courage as a lion tamer. He informed the people gathered around about the time when she had tamed one of the fiercest tigers to come out of Africa. They all pooled their money and entered.

The tiger began to lay down and yawn, once more revealing his toothless jaws. It was only the noise of the whip that disturbed him and kept him awake. "He must be a very old tiger," shouted Janie. The trumpets blared once more and it was over. Milly said, "We ought to ask for our money back."

"Look at her!" exclaimed Ted. "Who would be brave enough, or daft enough to try."

August Harrison, was a simple lad. He was not much to look at as far as looks were concerned. He had one peculiar feature – his eyes. One was a deep brown and the other blue. No one thought he was the marrying kind, for all the local girls laughed at him. So when rumors began to circulate that he was soon to marry a gypsy girl, no one could believe it. His father seemed rather downcast these days. He was far from being his usual self. Indeed, he was becoming very uncommunicative regarding his affairs in general.

One day, when August happened to be in the local shop, Mrs. Bamford said jokingly, "When's the lucky day?" He blushed and stuttered, but finally blurted out that he was already married. Naturally, she wanted all the news. Apparently, the union had been solemnized in the local church. Also a special gypsy wedding had been held. He showed the cut on his wrist to confirm this.

There was one on his wife's wrist also, so that the blood could be mingled. "Sounds like an old Hun custom," said Mrs. Bamford. "I think it was called Blood- Brotherhood, or something like that."

After the gypsies had been round for some time, people entertained the hope that they would soon move on. Their noisy presence in pubs and other public places was proving a great nuisance to the local residents. Since their arrival, the incidences of house burglaries were on the increase. Chickens left to roam in backyards began to disappear. The blame for this was put on the gypsies. So all in all the village people had had enough when a brawl broke out, many suffered minor cuts and bruises.

"You devils and witches!" yelled one bandy legged old man. He charged towards them followed by others. The fight was of a very short duration, for Colonel Upjohn had already summoned the police.

The following day, the police called on Farmer, Harrison to find out if he wanted any of the in-laws to stay. He shook his head. They informed him that the gypsies were being made to move on. His son pleaded with him to let them stay, as his wife was now with child. She can stay, or you can go with them, he said. The next day they all left, including his 'wife', whom he was never to see again, leaving a broken hearted August. The village would breathe freely once more.

Chapter XL

The August school holidays were here again. It was three years since the Reynolds had left Plinters' Street to settle in the country. Since then there had been many changes. Rose had given birth to five healthy pups. Bill had left the gas works. He had not felt the same, since one of his mates, overcome by the heat, had crossed the safety line, and had been devoured by the hungry flames. He was now self-employed as "plumber and drain layer". He had enough contracts to keep him going for at least six months. He was, needless to say looking healthier and happier with his outdoor work.

The news regarding Teds' health was very good. Doctor Punjab, had announced that he was fit enough to attend school. One of his lungs was completely healed, although the other would be a little while longer. So it came to be that Ted started school at last. His fragile form was to attract the likes of the school bully Michael Dunn, being the coward he was he found him an easy target.

One day the girls were held back and each thought the other would take Ted home. So it was inevitable that Micheal Dunn, the school bully, used this opportunity to have a go at Ted as he always hated the Reynolds girls. On reaching home the girls were told that Ted had not arrived. They retraced their steps and found poor Ted lying under a bush. Bill came home took one look at his son and shook his head.

"That damn bully must be stopped" he exclaimed

When Bill arrived home the next day he was in possession of a mysterious white box. The children gathered around him to see what was in it and he called Janie over to come closer. From the box he took a pair of red boxing gloves. Bill had been a champion boxer in the army.

"Now my girl, every evening when I come home, I will teach you how to defend yourself, and in doing so, you will be able to defend your brother and others like him. Said Jack

So began many hours of training, Bill got on his knees and would plead for Janie to punch him in the nose; it took some while before Janie took him up on his word. When she did, she delivered such a punch as to make Bill's nose bleed. She was scared at what she had done , but Bill hugged her.

" Well done Janie, now our training is complete."

Michael Dunn had behaved himself for a while until his mother sent him to the Bamford Store to get some groceries. He saw Ted standing in front of his house, he was waiting for George to come home; he seized the opportunity to attack him again. Bill, who was just coming around the corner of the house, saw him and called for Janie.

Michael Dunn was still beating Ted when she arrived. She launched him a blow and he fought back. By now people had gathered around to watch. Even the shopkeepers, the Bamfords had come out to watch "a girl fight the school bully?" one of them muttered in amazement.

Janie knew how to dodge a punch and get one in; what a fight it was. Suddenly Dunn broke away and started to run, he saw George making his way home and decided to land him a punch to help him on his way. Poor George received a mighty blow to his stomach which lifted him off the ground and onto his back. At the sight of this there was a sudden shout from the crowd. Janie was in hot pursuit after him, she chased him to the front door of his home; he tried closing the door on her but to no avail. The fight continued under the kitchen table, all the time his mother was yelling for the police and calling her a wicked child.

"My boy wouldn't hurt anyone," she screamed

Janie emerged from under the kitchen table the victor, her dress was torn and the bruise on her right eye was promising to be a shiner. The bully had at last met his match and what is more he was beaten by a girl.

From that day on Janie was known as the "bully shield" protector of all kids in her school – just as her father had intended.

Another Billy goat had now joined the Nanny goat. He was very proud of himself and possessed long horns. Bill had contrived a sledge, and when the snow lay thick on the ground in winter, the children had great fun sliding down the hills with old Billy pulling the sledge.

The world news told of the Reichstag fire and Hitler's successful bid for supreme power in Germany. Also, an airship had crashed with appalling loss of life. These events seemed so far away, and removed from the quiet life of the village.

Unconcerned though, by world events, young Janie was now looking forward to spending a week at Grandma's in London.

The prospect of Grandma ever visiting her daughter in the country was extremely remote. People living in vast urban areas tended to become hidebound and stuck within a limited radius, which included friends and relatives, and of course, the local pub. Here it was the custom to forgather for the purpose of exchanging tidbits of gossip over a glass of milk stout. This close-knit community was, as a rule, the extent of their horizon. Through the open door, Janie could discern such a group of middle aged women, sitting round a marble table. As she paused to look in, her shadow in the sunlight fell across the table, making them turn to look. At the sight of her, they began to reminisce on bygone days of their own youth. Janie passed on to wait at the traffic lights before crossing, a short distance past. As she waited to cross, she could hear their shrill laughter emanating from the stuffy confines of the pub.

After walking down two long streets, she turned onto Grenfell Street, and came to a high block of flats opposite a large playing field, where in were playing many children, yelling at the top of their voices for the ball to be thrown their way. Passing the first block of flats, she saw a group standing in front of the entrance of the second. They laughed and jeered as she approached, but were stopped by a tall youth, who had recognized her, and greeted her warmly.

"Why didn't you write and say you were coming? I would have arranged to meet you," he said.
"But mum did write and you were to have met me," replied Janie somewhat haughtily.

"I know nothing about this. Mum must have forgotten," Sid replied.

"Show me your flat," she ordered. Eagerly he obeyed.

The never ending stairway made Janie think of her Bible lessons at Sunday School, with the story of the Tower of Babel. On finally reaching the flat, Sid produced a key and opened the door. The front door opened up into a large hall, which ran the length of the flat, with two bedrooms either side, bathroom and kitchen on the right opposite a dining room-come-lounge. It was indeed surprisingly large and spacious, the walls been painted in pastel shades.

She was to share a room with her mother's youngest sister, who had just turned eighteen. Putting her case down, she couldn't help noticing two extremely large pictures on the wall. One of an Angel ascending into heaven, the other, showing numerous Angels flying through the sky. She felt oddly fascinated and repelled by them and hurried from the room. Sid had meanwhile prepared some afternoon tea for her, for which she was grateful. The journey she felt had been long and her first alone.

Sounds of laughter and noise from heavy square heeled shoes heralded the approach of his mother, in company with other people. An instant later the door opened and she made her appearance. She was followed by her friends as they came into the dining room. She was full of good cheer, having, no doubt, downed a few Guinness' during the course of the morning.

"A friend of yours?" she remarked to Sid, glancing in Janie's direction. "It's polite to introduce people, you know."

"Oh yes mum, beg your pardon and all that, but this happens to be Janie, you know, Victoria's girl.

"Goodness me, so you're our Janie! Victoria's child. I'd never have recognized you. My, you certainly have grown Janie. That country air has done wonders for you. Oh, but I forgot, nobody met you at the station."

"That's alright Grandma," said Janie, "I managed to find my way. I was given directions on how to get here by the station porter."

"Oh, but your mum and dad would never forgive me if they knew." She collapsed into the nearest chair and so did her friends. She showed great interest in Janie, asking her many questions about life in the country, vowing one day to come and see them. Janie smiled to herself, knowing full well that Grandma would not budge beyond the radius of a quarter of a mile or so. Many like her, would survive the London Blitz and still stay put.

"Goodness gracious me!" said Grandma, "time for tea." This had the effect of setting her in motion, which, in turn, had a disturbing effect on her cronies, who forthwith began to make excuses for leaving, as they had much work to do at home. They waddled like a pack of penguins to the front door and were not too long in making their exits.

Very soon the door bell began to ring again as various members of the family returned home from work. Alf entered first, followed very soon after by George, Ernie, Terrance, Harry and Janie's favourite, Uncle Charlie. They all kissed and hugged her in turn, as they were all happy to see her. They were anxious to know how the rest of the family was and promised to be down again to see them on the next long holiday weekend. Ablutions were proceeded with before tea began, resulting in a mad scamper for the bathroom, ending up in playful fights in the hall, until Annie's Grandma's shrill voice could be heard remonstrating above the commotion. They would then turn their attention on her, and lifting her small form high above their shoulders, they carried her high in the air, until she was begging to be put down, sorry that she had told them off.

Janie could see that she enjoyed every minute of it as the scene, with others just as delightful, was to be repeated many times during the rest of her stay with Grandma. They were all very fond of her, and one formed the impression that there was nothing they would not do for her within their capacity and reasonable limits.
.

Terrance, who was to be married, had to go for a fitting for his suit. George was to go dancing with his fiancé and the two who were already married, Ernest and Harry, left to return home to their wives. The others went out, as it was a fine summer evening, to the playing field opposite, for a game of football with their friends. Watching them from the window, Janie wondered at their energy, for they had all put in a gruelling eight hours in some factory or other.

Granddad arrived home with an abundant supply of vegetables' and a large bunch of fragrant pinks, her favorite flowers. He kissed Janie very fondly, being, overjoyed to have her staying with them for a week, and said he wished it could be much longer, for they saw very little of them since they took to living in the country. He allowed her to arrange the flowers in the vases for him, and promised he would take her to see his allotment, situated near the gasworks, before she returned home. Janie's family often discussed Granddad at home. He was one of the old- school gentlemen. He took life as it came. He was never known to have said a harsh word to or about anyone. He had known better times, but was always ready to accept the precept that one must be prepared to give as well as to receive in this world of ours. Janie grew to love him, the more she knew of him and was always prompt to give him a helping hand whenever it was required of her.

Granddad was always a gentleman. He came from a very wealthy family; it was said that they owned an enormous amount of horses and that they were involved in the selling of wholesale meat. In the First World War, the government took most of the horses to the front line and so ruined the family business.

She retired early to bed that evening. Doris had not yet arrived home as the others had done. Apparently, she was dining out with a young man. For a while, the visions of the strange pictures on the wall kept her awake, but before long she had fallen asleep.

She was startled out of her slumber by the light being suddenly switched on. She lay transfixed as it were. Her heart was literally pounding - ensuing bodily pulsations, generated feelings of nausea. Doris, unaware of Janie's discomfort, took her to be still asleep, after greeting her and getting no answer.

Doris had much to occupy her thoughts. At the moment she was thinking of Dennis's offer of marriage that evening. But oh, the thought of being irrevocably tied down – sort of being owned by someone. She was used to having everything her own way, for after all, she had left school at the age of fourteen, and had worked during the past four years in a cigarette factory. Yes, the thought of losing her independence certainly had a daunting effect on her. She climbed into bed, and lying on her back, she vacantly watched the moon on its journey through the heavens. Sleep eventually overtook her troubled mind.

Chapter XLI

When Janie woke up the next morning, Doris had already left for work. She was sorry to have missed her. She recalled how ill she felt on being woken up during the night, and hoped that such an experience would not be repeated.

Janie insisted on helping with the household chores and was given the job of scrubbing the wooden shelves of the walk-in food pantry, after having first tidied up the bedrooms. She found that Grandma had worked quickly and expertly through the flat, leaving them plenty of time throughout the day to themselves. She offered to take her to the cinema. Mother had already told Janie that Grandma did not esteem the cinema as entertainment, preferring real people to celluloid ones. Janie loved to see the good Rin-tin-tin dog films and Charlie Chaplin, which were hardly Grandma's type.

They were sitting down to lunch when Janie was startled by a noise that sounded like a ricochet of bullets hitting the window. Hurriedly getting up from her seat Grandma commenced to make a number of sandwiches, and putting them into a brown paper bag, crossed the room to the window. Opening it, she threw the bag out. Janie, who had been watching the proceedings, not without a little puzzlement, remained quiet. It was considered in bad taste to be constantly asking adults why they did this and why they did that. Instead, she got on with her lunch, conversation not being encouraged by the elders.

The day passed pleasantly enough. Sid returned earlier than usual and asked to play a game of tennis with her. She accepted, but on entering the grounds, they were surrounded by his school friends and he was sidetracked into a game of football instead. Bouncing her ball against the wooden fence, she soon became bored and headed for home. On the way back she passed a strange looking boy. She noticed that his head was extra large. Taking little notice of her, he limped past her on the stairway.

Grandma's cronies called early the following morning, a little after breakfast. This entailed the consumption of many cups of tea. It had the effect of putting the house out of routine, and many of the jobs fell to her to do.

It came to lunchtime, and no lunch had been prepared. The pebbles began to pound the windows again, but it seemed that Janie was the only one who heard it. She went to the window to look out; it was a long way down. Half afraid, she made to withdraw, but was hailed by the strange boy she had passed the other day.

"Mrs Holder," he called, "Hammer go twice!!"

"What do you want?" shouted Janie back at him.

"Hammer go twice!!" he replied.

Puzzled, she withdrew, and went over to tell Grandma, whose immediate reaction was to make sandwiches and so repeating the daily ritual.

It was three o'clock when Janie saw her way clear to visit the store, to spend her pocket money, and buy a few items for Grandma. Turning out of Grenfell Street into Durban Road, she reached the shop and walked in. She spent a lot of time just looking and asking the price of this and that item. The shopkeeper was kind and patient.

"You're new around here?" he asked.

"I'm staying with my Grandmother for a short while, Mrs Holder," replied Janie.

"Mrs Holder, ah yes, I know her well. They're good people. And what's your name, might I ask?" He was asking this question just as two older girls made their appearance in the shop.

"My name is Janie Reynolds."

The two girls began to look curiously at her, and then to talk quietly among themselves. They made their purchases and left the shop. She could not make up her mind as to what to buy, but instead confined herself to making Grandma's purchases. When she got outside, she found the two girls she had seen in the shop now waiting for her. One shyly approached her.

"I heard you say that you were Janie Reynolds." Surprised, Janie nodded. "Well, I'm Ivy Felton, your cousin. We heard from Sid that you were staying a week in London. Do come home with us. This is my sister Lilly, we live a few houses down this street."

The houses had a monotonous appearance about them;

all had round bay windows, upstairs and down. The doors were barely perceptible under a gloomy porch. Only the numbers were different. Number ten had the same chipped paint, weather beaten look. Most had lace curtains, just like Plinters Street, and like Plinters Street, dark inside. So dark, in fact, that it was normal to have a gas mantle lit all day to show the way up the hall.

When they arrived, a fat woman, with the sleeves of her dress rolled up, was undressing a child to bathe him. A younger woman was pouring warm water into a small galvanised bath that stood on a large wooden table, almost filling the room. Looking round, once her eyes became accustomed to the gloom, Janie noticed a number of people in the room of various ages. They had all stopped what they were doing to look at her. Feeling shy at being the centre of attention, Janie stood awkwardly near the table. The fat woman commenced her operations at the bath, and got on with bathing the baby, but taking time to cast long dull looks in her direction. Also further adding to her discomfort, were the attentions given to her by a large bright green, red and yellow parrot, with a monstrously curved beak and very wicked looking eyes. He was looking at her through the wire cage which only just contained him. Then in a high pitched chatter, he began calling her fowl names and swearing in the most shocking and bizarre manner.

"Go home you f... bitch, Go home!! Go home!! Jack!! Jack!! F... Bitch!!" screamed the Parrot at Janie

A dried up looking man shouted at him, "Look here, that's no way to speak to a lady." Hiding his head in his feathers, the muffled reply came back,

"Sorry Jack, sorry!!"

The steam from the bath was getting into her hair, making it feel damp. She put her hand up to brush away the few strands that had fallen over her eyes. Then the creature suddenly went mad biting off another stream of abuse at her. If he ever succeeded in getting out, she thought, he would claw me to pieces. Instinctively she moved away from the cage. Noticing her apparent discomfort, the old man rose from his chair and fetching a large cloth, he immediately covered the cage. The parrot looked contritely at him saying

"I said I was sorry didn't I!!"

Janie noticed at that moment a certain likeness and, as it were, kinship between him and the parrot. The irony of the situation suddenly made her to break out laughing. This caused the ice to break, and the fat woman seemed to regard her in a more favourable light. Ivy nodded in her direction, with her somewhat tardy introduction.

"Mum, this is Janie, you know, Uncle Bill's girl."

"Well bless my soul, you don't say, so you're my brother's little girl."

She nodded towards the cage,

"You must not mind 'im, he's been thirteen years on a cargo boat with 'ole Jack 'ere."

The words uttered by the woman took a little while to register, as Janie could not associate her by any stretch of imagination, with that of her father; for hadn't he spoken of a young and pretty girl who had once taken care of him when he had fled from the trenches of France during the Great War. He had enlisted, in a state of patriotic fervour, making out to be older than he was at the time; only living to regret his untimely eviction. When the military police had finally caught up with him, he had succeeded meanwhile in joining another regiment, and by the time he was to be posted once more to the trenches, the armistice had been concluded.

It seemed she had suddenly acquired so many more cousins in the space of one short hour. No one bothered to explain why she had not already met them before this date. They asked her to stay to tea, but she declined on this occasion, as Grandma had urged her to hurry home, and would by now be worried about her. She thanked them for their offer and promised to pay them another visit before she returned home.

Ivy and Lily, both attractive girls, had the pale colouring of the city dwellers. Even in Summer most of the sunshine was lost on them, as they had to spend a lot of their time between walls of grim Victorian school buildings. Both girls saw her to the gate to bid her farewell until she should visit them again, which they hoped, was fairly soon. Janie noticed, on departure, the hand spun heavy laced curtains in the house next door had parted, revealing the extremely pale, but beautiful face of a girl about her own age. Her features were finely wrought, as if executed by the finest of sculptors, a hand as delicate as the child's descended on her shoulders and gently drew her away.

She was to learn later that a woman and child had moved into the premises a number of years ago. The child had never been seen going to school, or for that matter, was rarely ever seen at all. The grocer had been instructed to leave all deliveries on the porch, from whence the cash, which was left out, was collected. People were heard to say that they were never visited by anyone. Janie's mind was haunted by the almost ghostly smile she had seen on her face for a long time afterwards.

That evening back in Grandma's past much as usual, Uncle Charlie, the one who had once contributed money for flower seeds at Laindon Hill now found little jobs for her to do. It gave him the excuse to keep her in pocket money. She knew he did this because she was brought up to accept money only for effort of some kind.

She had also met Doris several times since she arrived. She had shampooed her hair, and had taught her the art of using lipstick and face powder. She also let her borrow one of her dresses, and a pair of high-heeled shoes. With her hair set high upon her head, she really began to feel grown up. They all played up to her imagination, and duly flattered her.

Chapter XLII

Today was Friday, she was to leave for home on Sunday. Grandma was out doing the shopping and Janie had promised to clean the pantry. The sound of a small pebbles hitting the window, reminded her of the daily ritual. The strange looking boy was again demanding:

"Hammer go Twice!!" "Hammer go twice!!"

Going to the pantry, she searched for bread with which to make his sandwiches, as she had seen the others do. But this time, Grandma had forgetfully put the unwanted food on to the chute which led to the garbage bin at floor level. She spotted a half loaf of bread on the very top shelf which seemed to have been overlooked. Getting it down, she tried to cut it into slices, but was unsuccessful as the bread was too hard. It must have been on the shelf for some time, for it was rock hard. Putting it down again, she returned to the window, the boy was still standing there, but growing impatient.

"Mrs Holder is out," Janie called.

Impatiently he answered;

"Hammer go Twice!!" "Hammer Go Twice!!"

She returned to the pantry and the stale bread. Well anything is better than nothing, she murmured. Going to the open window, she called out to the boy and threw the bread down to him. On its rapid decent, passing one floor after another, a head popped out, just in time to receive a resounding blow. Bouncing off, it fell to the ground below, where it was eagerly pounced upon by the starving Hammer, who carrying it off to the nearby park, sat down and struggled hard to get his teeth into it. He seemed to be enjoying it, for his was a case of true and dedicated hunger.

The whole incident would never have come to light if it hadn't been for one of Grandma's cronies, who's head the bread had struck. As soon as she came back from her shopping the woman wasted no time in lodging her complaint. She was angry with Janie, and told her that when next Hammer called on her, she was to walk to the shop with him. By afternoon, he must have been hungry, for this time he climbed the many flights of steps and pressed the doorbell button. True to her word, Grandma hit upon some item she wanted, and Janie in the company of Hammer, were despatched to the shop, the corner shop, where the former had met her cousins the other day. Considering his bad limp, Hammer walked very quickly, and Janie found it a task to keep pace with him. She was searching her mind for something to say to him, in atonement for her behaviour towards him that morning. He turned his large soft eyes to meet her gaze. She gathered that he must be somewhat older than he looked. As if reading her mind, he said,

"Hammer did enjoy the bread." Shame filled her.

"I really am sorry," she said and meant it.

They were to become firm friends for the rest of her stay. She was to glean the meaning of the phrase 'Hammer Go Twice'. He would throw the pebbles at the window about lunch time as a signal that he wanted to eat. In the afternoon, he knocked on the doors to run errands, in order to obtain food and money for his family, to whom she was soon to be introduced.

One time Grandma had baked a large pie, and Janie and Hammer had to take it to the Latter's family. The flat in which they lived was situated on the top floor on the next, but one block. On entering, she witnessed a sight which made her heart contract painfully. The doors of adjoining rooms were all opened up, revealing the dire poverty in which the family was living. There was sacking, apparently used as bedding, placed in layers on the floors of two rooms. The third contained an old rusty iron bed, containing a very grubby looking mattress, on which lay a sick and badly deformed man, covered by a very ragged old coat. Close by, sitting on an orange box, was a small woman with enormous legs. There were three other children all younger than Hammer. The youngest was sitting on the floor, part covered in faecal matter. Scattered around the floor were dozens of old newspapers. The whole place exuded a cacophony of malodorous smells, emanating, no doubt, from this gross commingling of papers, faeces and decaying pieces of food left lying about.

The woman sized the proffered pie without saying a word. Breaking it into pieces with her hands, she gave a piece to each child and kept a piece for herself. She noticed that nothing was saved for the sick man or Hammer. Completely disregarding her, they set to and devoured the pie. She felt her hand gently taken, and Hammer led her to the front door and out from a scene that both sickened and saddened her. Halfwit that he was, he was endeavouring to keep his family alive, Janie succeeded in wiping the tears away. Hammer left her to continue with his errands.

Sid let her in. When she saw Grandma, she told her everything she had seen. Grandma perceived her distress, and was at pains to explain to her that they and others were doing their best to help the family. "We try to hold the family together, for if they should finish up in the workhouse, the man would be separated from his wife." She convinced Janie that there were many caring people in the neighbourhood who were prepared to go to any lengths to see that those less fortunate than themselves were taken care of and not allowed to go cold and hungry.

Saturday was to find her in the company of her youngest uncle, Sid, in the cinema. They had been watching a Charlie Chaplin film. As the lights began to dim, for the second half, all the young people in the place began to cheer as their dog hero, Rin Tin Tin, made his appearance on the screen. He held them to the end with his long display of daring escapades.

Too soon, it was over.

"Well worth the threepence," commented Sid.

They blinked their eyes, as they came out into full daylight. When they reached Durban Road, she asked him if he would accompany her to the Feltons, whom she had promised to visit that day. He shook his head, he was to meet his mates at the park for a round of football.

Janie was greeted warmly by the Feltons, and this time was able to accept their offer of staying to tea. During the course of the meal, there came a knock at the door. There was, for reasons unknown to her, a great hush on the assembly. No one appeared to want to move, much to her puzzlement.

"Better answer it, Mary," said the dried up old man.

"I haven't the money to pay him Jack. Ivy dear, you answer it, will yer. It's the insurance man. Tell him I'm not in. Tell him, I'll pay him in three weeks time." Ivy went to the door at her mother's request. Everyone in the room sat hushed and rooted to their chairs as the door was opened, waiting for Ivy to speak.

"Mum said she ain't in, and she'll pay you in three weeks time."

"Oh she did, did she. Well you go right back and tell her I want to see her this very minute!!" Replied the insurance man.

A crestfallen look crossed the woman's face and reaching into the pocket of her apron, she pulled out an old, worn and somewhat battered black purse. Opening it, she searched out six shillings, and angrily passed it over to her erring daughter.

"Here, take it and pay him. I'll deal with you later," she muttered.

Ivy reached across for the payments book on the mantelpiece and went out to pay the waiting man, who was wearing a sarcastic sneer on his face.

"You see," he was heard to say, "It ain't quite so painful after all. I'll be back again in another fortnight. Good day to you."

Every one continued with their tea once again as Ivy came in to place the payments book back on the shelf. They all watched her in silence. Somebody was heard to say, 'dunderhead'. Ivy replied to this defiantly,

"Well, mum did say she was out."

Janie enjoyed the evening, with no abuse from the parrot, for he was covered up. Twilight was beginning to fall as she bade them all farewell. Her Aunt brought out her black purse, opening it, she took out a silver florin. She declined to accept it, as she thought the family must be very hard up, after what she had witnessed. But her glance fell on the large open purse. She could not believe her eyes when she saw a roll of crisp pound notes buried inside. On looking round the room she made a quick calculation, at least five of them must be working. Her aunt was now pressing five shillings on her. "Something to share with your brothers and sisters," she said. Janie, knowing it would be rude to continue refusing was able to accept the money without any further qualms. She kissed her

Aunt goodbye.

"Come again," they all said, as she left them. "We'll meet again soon." Ivy called as Janie neared the corner. Turing she waved and disappeared from sight.

Chapter XLIII

On Sunday morning, Granddad took her, as he had promised, to his allotment by the gasworks. An allotment in this case, meant a parcelling up of spare land, not available for immediate development, for letting out at a modest rental to employees of the company. Each plot of ground, revealed much of a man's character, in the arrangement of vegetables and flowers, the proportion of one thing grown to another, and it's degree of tidiness. Some plots, which were bordering the giant cylinders, had various plants climbing up them, it was man and nature trying to come to terms in an effort to cover the formers ugly creations, but not quite succeeding.

Granddad's pinks and carnations, his favourite flowers made a brilliant splash of colour, and the aroma held one's nostrils captivated - a splash of heaven, thrown amongst mankind's vanities. He had brought some scissors with him, and cutting some of his choice blooms, he laid them in her arms.

"Now, you look like a princess. Think you'll be able to manage the marrow Janie?" She nodded behind it's immensity.

Granddad laughed at the incongruity of the situation – little Janie, carrying a marrow almost her own size! She was so anxious to show her dad what a great gardener Granddad was.

"Have you enjoyed your stay with us?" he asked.

"Yes thank you, it's been most interesting." She meant it.

The family was foregathered on the platform, waiting for the train Janie was to be on, to make its appearance. The whistling steam train pulled into the station. The waiting crowd began picking up their luggage and forming themselves into little groups, hoping they would be in line with a carriage door when the train finally came to a grinding halt.

 Janie's family waited eagerly for her to make an appearance, but so far there was no sign of her. Feeling worried that she might have missed the train, Bill began walking up the platform in search for her. "There she is!" Indeed it was her alright, although a bit bedraggled, and almost obscured by her Granddad's giant marrow, and a huge cascade of choice flowers. He came up behind her, and playfully tugged at her golden curls. She giggled as he pulled one of his funny faces, causing her to drop the marrow. He whistled as he pick it up. "What a beauty! One of your Granddad's I bet."

As the platform was fast emptying, the rest of the family could now easily be seen formed into a group near the ticket collector who was a personal friend. They all greeted her as if she had been away for years, instead of just one week. She felt overjoyed at their warmth and love and only just began to realise how much she had missed them all. She hugged her mother, brothers and sister, showing how she was glad to be with them once more. Ted was impatient to show her 'something,' but Milly and Victoria delayed her by asking questions about their folks in London. George was swung up on dad's shoulders, and began to beam down at everybody with evident delight at them all. As they moved towards the exit, the friendly ticket collector waved them by and ruffled Janie's curls as she passed. They clambered up the wooden steps reaching the main road. Ted and Milly in company with Bill, who was still carrying George, ran on ahead. Victoria accompanied Janie, who could not understand why the former was walking at such a slow pace. "Get a move on Mum," said Janie impatiently, as the others were lost to sight.

When they finally emerged from the station into the street, she could hardly believe her eyes, when she saw that the others were now seated in a trap, harnessed up to a beautiful ginger coloured pony. Everyone was grinning, waiting to see her reaction. They were not disappointed, as Janie was both surprised and very thrilled by what she saw. The pony snorted and raised his head as she attempted to stroke his nose. "Dad, he's beautiful, is he ours?" Bill nodded in evident satisfaction.

"Yes Janie, he is ours alright. Hop in and I'll take you for a ride."
"What's his name dad," she asked.
"That's for you children to decide," he replied.

They assisted her into the carriage. Victoria took her place in front next to Bill, who was now making a clicking sound with his mouth. With a shake of the reins, they set off on a ride round Laindon Hills. Taking in great gulps of the clean fresh air, Janie could not help comparing the peace and tranquillity of this place, with the noise and bustle of London. She sat quietly drinking it all in.

Chapter XLIV

It all began at the tea table. The family had been laughing at some of Janie's narratives of amusing events, during her stay in London. Ted, who had been laughing with the rest, suddenly went into convulsions and becoming blue in the face. He had put a halfpenny into his mouth, apparently thinking it was food. He was now fighting for his breath. Bill acted quickly, by opening his mouth to blow down his throat. It was then that he noticed the halfpenny embedded in the boy's throat. The events which followed took on the aspect of a nightmare to the Reynolds. Bill tried to extricate the coin covering the windpipe. He even tipped him upside-down. Ted was looking very ill, and on the point of death. Milly and Janie clung to each other, too scared to speak. The halfpenny had moved a fraction, enough at least to let some air into the boy's lungs. He continued to blow into his mouth, at the same time, calling to Victoria to harness the pony and trap. Fortunately, as it turned out, it was still harnessed. Bill ran, with the boy in his arms and got in, bidding Victoria to take over the reins and drive for all she was worth. It was indeed a matter of life and death. She was skilled with horses, having been brought up with them as a young girl. Also, she had to drive a team of four horses with carriage, at a college for young ladies during the beginning of the First World War.

With Victoria in full command, the pony and trap literally streaked off down the road. It was a number of miles to the hospital. Still huddled together, and crying silently the children went inside the house, not knowing if they would ever see their brother alive again. "Please God," pleaded Janie to herself, "Please save our brother."

The mad dash to the hospital seemed never ending to the frantic parents. Accidents were avoided by her skilful handling of the pony. On reaching the hospital, Bill ran through the entrance and had waylaid the nearest nurse and had begun pleading with her when a young doctor fresh on night duty happened to be passing at the time. He was able to take the matter in hand immediately, and after a few minutes expert manipulation, was able to extirpate the offending article. "Not before time," exclaimed the doctor. "We'll have to keep him in for a few hours observation."

"We can stay with him, can we?"
"Most certainly, you can." Ted had by now recovered, having got the colour back into his face again. "My, you're a lucky boy," said the doctor. He handed the coin back to Bill, who noticed that it had turned green.

Victoria had been quietly crying all this time. Bill looked at her, and observed how spent she looked. "Cheer up girl," he was saying. "As soon as we get home, you can relax for the rest of the evening in the armchair, and I'll brew a nice pot of tea for us." He was slightly hoarse as he thanked the doctor in this usual gruff way. People were aware that he wore his heart on his sleeve, no matter how hard he tried to conceal the fact. On reaching home, they found George asleep, also the girls huddled together asleep on the old settee.

Chapter XLV

Winter rains had begun, and inclement muddy conditions made it impossible for Bill to continue with his work. He would be forced to take a break until the better weather came again. At least, he could collect his overdue accounts, for many people were owing money for work carried out during the busy summer months. Also, he had accounts of his own to pay, which could only be met by the money he would have to collect. His charges for installing sewerage connections had been very reasonable, and what was more, his work was hailed as being first class. During the time he had set out to work for himself he had achieved great personal satisfaction. "Tomorrow," he informed his wife, "I'll go round and collect some money due to me."

"And not before time either," chided Victoria, "Our creditors aren't prepared to wait much longer." Taking 'Halfpenny' (so he had been named) the pony, he harnessed him up, and set off early, bubbling over with good humour. Already he was thinking what could be done with the surplus cash, provided of course, that everyone paid up. A crestfallen man entered the house many hours later, many of his clients were unable to pay him, and the way things were going, he would barely cover his own bills. The worst offenders were those people who paraded a facade of wealth and snobbery, and where the lady of the house would parade the streets in an expensive fur coat, but could not afford to pay their most elementary accounts. Those with the latest model motor cars in their garage, were the most unconscionable about paying their bills, and would use every unscrupulous method in the book to get out of paying them. Against people like these, poor Bill stood not an earthly chance.

It was working people, he discovered, people who struggled, like himself, who paid up. These people were indeed the backbone of England, and if they ever faltered or went down, so too, would England. They were to prove their mettle later on, when the war came.

Bill sat very depressed for a while, but suddenly brightened up. There was one person he had forgotten, and who's payment would tip the scales quite considerably in his favour. This person owed him a large sum of money, for he had received no progress payments from her. She had always insisted on plying him with food and drink and had often bestowed on him, a jar of jam, or home made toffee to take home to his family. Such a person surely, he thought, would not quibble about paying up.

"Yes! Mrs Brinkwater!" Bill muttered allowed to himself.

She greeted him in her usual way, insisting as usual upon plying him with a cup of tea and biscuits. She assured him beyond any doubt that she would indeed pay him; if he would call the following Friday. However, when he returned to the pleasant Mrs Brinkwater's house, on the appointed day, he was met at the door by complete strangers. They knew nothing about the unpaid bill, having just bought the house, and had no idea where she had moved too. But they could tell him the 'agent' who sold them the house. Who it seemed was unable, or rather, as Bill surmised, did not want to give out information, his job was done.

"How can I?" he said to Victoria later on, "Get money from people, who either cannot pay or do not want to pay me."

The children looked sadly in his direction as he sat smoking his pipe by the kitchen stove.

When Colonel Upjohn heard of his plight, he was

indignant, "Don't trust the buggers," he had often warned Jack, "I'll do what I can to help find you a job. I know many people." And he was as good as his word. Jack ended up a wiser man.

Chapter XLVI

Mr York detested his present way of living. He felt utterly jaded. There were times when he felt he could not face another day and wondered what on earth had possessed him to take up the teaching profession. It was slowly, by degrees driving him mad. Some people were born to teach, but he well knew by now that he was not in that sublime category. Politics, he was sure, would have suited him better with his unscrupulous inclinations.

He took in the rows of bent heads. What could one really choose between them. Surely it was a waste of time trying to educate them. In his opinion they were all a dead loss. Judging by the way things were going in Europe, they would soon be engulfed by the most terrible war ever waged. The grim prognosis of the powers that be, was that air raids carried out by armadas of air planes would virtually destroy whole cities and wipe out their populations. What, indeed, was he educating them for anyway, when they were all soon to die.

Again, his eyes travelled slowly over the rows of bent heads until they came to rest on one particular pupil, one of the scapegoats of his mounting rancour. He could not abide that cockney kid, Janie Reynolds. He noticed though, that she seemed to be deeply immersed in a book. Perhaps, he thought, something was getting through into that thick skull of hers. He would see. Breaking the silence suddenly, he spoke,

"So Janie, you know all about the Wars of the Roses do you? Janie, you can stand up and tell me, who were the warring factions, and who won the war- if indeed wars are ever won"

Poor Janie felt painfully severed from the events of the narrative she had been reading. Nervously she bit her bottom lip. The teacher's eyes narrowed to slits,

"Come child now, some of the contents of the book must have penetrated that fat head of yours."

Her teeth sank deeper into her lip, further restricting the flow of blood, rendering it a sickly white colour, but her cheeks glowed deep red. He strode angrily to the back of the room, where she stood. Snatching at the book on the desk, he picked it up. His eyes widened, as a look of incredulity spread over his face. Waving the book wildly in the air, he placed his hand on her arm, at the same time sinking his fingers viciously into her tender skin, and began dragging her up to the front of the class.

"So you little brat, you thought you'd make a fool of me did you?" Dropping the book, he shook her till her teeth began to rattle. "I'll show you my girl, I'll show you!"

She pulled away from his cruel hold on her, and stood looking proud and defiant. Her action inflamed his temper even more, and picking up the book, he threw it at her. It caused a resounding blow against Janie's chest causing her to reel backwards. For reasons unknown to her, Janie tried to arrest the book from falling on the floor.

"Tell the class what book you chose to read during your history lesson, you obstinate child, go on, face the class and tell them." Still proud and defiant, she faced them all. Speaking loud and clear, she told them,

"David Copperfield; written by Charles Dickens."

Snatching the book away from her, he put his face close to hers. She smelt the odour of tobacco in his hot breath, which stung her face as he spoke,

"There's no future for the likes of you. Sit down."

She could still feel the sensation of his grip upon her arm as she sat for a long time afterwards, for the pain lingered on, the physical pain served to emphasise the degree of mental pain she was having to endure. By now, many of the pupils, who had been quickly scanning their history texts, had their hands in the air, eager to show off their scant, but briefly held knowledge.

The bell rang for home time. Just as Janie was leaving the classroom, Mr York called on her to remain behind. She was to clean the blackboard, put the chairs up and sweep the classroom floor. And further, she was to write out a hundred lines stating, 'I must always obey my teacher'. To Janie, this held a nasty sloganish sound, but she could not determine its source.

All was very quiet when she finished. She noticed the portly figure of the headmaster, as he went round locking up, but he did not even spare her the merest glance. As far as he was concerned, she thought she did not even exist. Very despondently, she closed the gate after her, crossed the road and followed the rough footpath until it reached the lane that wound its way to her home.

Chapter XLVII

Victoria at that moment was waiting beside a large Bentley sports car, whose owner should have been back by now. If he did not very soon come, she would have to start walking home. Two big soft eyed spaniels were waiting patiently with her. They did not realise at the time, their doggy minds did not comprehend, that their master was not to take them on another shooting trip, at least not for a long time to come.

The staff at the hotel had of course heard about the quarrel between the young proprietors during the night. The following morning was to find them sleeping in separate rooms. There were many amused comments about this, as the couple had not long been married.

His father had bought the lovely hotel as a wedding gift for them. They were now walking towards her. Victoria was thinking that 'Lady Luck' was indeed smiling on the pair of them. But on taking a closer look at the woman, she could detect the pouting lines of discontent firming round the mouth. That terrible scourge of an idle and effete society, ennui, was already apparent in her whole bearing. She was now standing beside her. They liked each other. Addressing Victoria with a smile, she asked her if she could see her way clear to working the weekend at the hotel. "We, my husband and I, that is, would like to spend a few days together away from everyone. Do you mind very much, Victoria?" She seemed to be pleading with her eyes, more than her voice. Victoria relayed to him that she would be more than happy to oblige.

The proprietor of the hotel drew up quietly outside her bungalow. As she moved to alight, he put a hand out to detain her, "How would you like to manage the hotel for us during the next week. I will give you Carte-Blanche Victoria." She felt reluctant at first to accept the challenge. All the same she accepted

"Yes Mr Lausbury, I'll do it," she said.

"Good, Victoria, I shall tell the staff that you are now in charge. I have every confidence in you." Waving her goodbye, he was soon out of sight.

The Davenport sisters arrived just as Bill brought Halfpenny and the trap round to the front of the house. They all climbed in and he turned the pony in the direction of Aunt Grace's cottage. They would pick up Brenda, despite his aversion for the girl. She saw them approaching and immediately rushed inside to pick up her school hat and bag. Brenda gave Halfpenny a big hug before getting into the trap. He snorted and whinnied his approval as they started out.

The girls chattered among themselves. Janie exclaimed excitedly, how much she was beginning to like high school. "I'll give you all a ride back when you finish school."

"That'll be great dad." He pulled up outside the school gates. When they had all alighted, he again began to grin slyly at them. "Dad, you must be up to something," said Milly.

"I'll be seeing you," he said, as the pony cantered away.

The tittering in the class began about mid-morning. Miss Jones turned round from the blackboard, it all seemed very silent. She assumed writing on the blackboard then it happened again. 'What can it be?' she thought, as she turned round once more. She could not believe her eyes. Framed as it were, in one of the side windows, was a distorted face. It was only there for a few seconds before it was to disappear from sight. Every pupil in the class was looking in that direction.

"Silence", she commanded. "Now what indeed is going on here. If I don't get better behaviour from you all, you can stop behind after school." She walked over to the window and looked out. She could see nobody. She returned to the blackboard. Hardly had her back been turned a few minutes, when the face returned once again, this time more grotesque than ever. There was a great peel of laughter. But this time she was prepared, and turning round quickly, beheld the face in all its contorted splendour. "Who is that man?" she shouted angrily. Janie bent her head over her desk, pretending not to have heard the question. But some of the children raised their hands. "Well," she asked.

"Please Miss, it's Janie's father, Mr Reynolds."
"Oh, it is, is it!" Well Janie Reynolds, go and tell him to get on with his job, and then perhaps I can get on with mine. Red faced, she left the room.

"Hello Janie, I think you've got a message for me."
"Yes dad, the teacher says you've got to stop pulling faces through the window."

"She did, did she, the old grump." The teacher was back writing on the blackboard as Janie took her seat. All eyes were on the window in anticipation of another showing. They were not to be disappointed, up came the head again showing a distorted visage, with tongue stuck out, pointing at the teacher's back. This time, she turned round, and went storming across the room to the window. She opened it and shouted,

"Mr Reynolds, if I may so name you. Do you think you can step in and do my job for me? I'm getting sick of your childish pranks outside my classroom." Looking up to her from the hole he was standing in, he said with mock respect,

"Now Miss, a little laughter doesn't hurt anyone, does it?" With eyes almost popping out of her head, she slammed the window shut, switched the lights on and drew the curtains.

At lunch time, a number of children gathered round the large hole that Bill was digging, asking him questions about his work. He was at pains to explain to them in as much detail as he could marshal about the laying of sewer pipes and the sewer system in general terms. At the end of the school session the Reynolds children were again treated to another lift home in the trap. This was to continue for the next few weeks, while their father was working on the school premises. Unfortunately, the pupils were not to be served up with any further entertainment, as the headmaster had given Jack a reprimanding for his unorthodox behaviour.

After a relaxing weekend at home, Victoria arrived back to work Monday morning to find that the army had taken residence in the hotel during her absence. Apparently, the reserves had been called up owing to the war scare. The dining room was to act as the H.Q. It had already been partly converted, as there were already clerks and typists at work.

Mr Lansbury was holding a conversation with the C.O. when Victoria arrived. He introduced her, "My good woman," he exclaimed, "You're the most important person here. All my officers and men have been marching since just before midnight. Could you prepare a meal for them as quickly as you can, they're starving! Would you undertake also, in future, the cooking and preparation of the Officers meals, the army cooks will take care of the rest."

Trestles and tables had already been commandeered by the army on instructions from the War Office. Extra beds had been placed in all rooms. Instructions had been issued to exclude civilians from the premises, except in bars.

The faces of the maids looked white and strained. Even Mr Grant, the head steward, was not his usual impeccable self. "Well," said Victoria, "War or no war, the men must be fed. Let's get to it!" Everyone, including the owner got tucked in, under her masterly supervision in preparing huge pots of tea and mountains of sandwiches.

The days that followed were hectic, but in a short while, a routine had finally been got under way. The men were constantly out on the march, engaged in firearms practice and foot drills, and eventually given a few hours leave. They would spend it locally filling up the cinemas and dance halls, and generally creating a diversion for the local people. Colonel Upjohn was in his element as he had a few old friends among the unit. Life also took on a special interest for single girls of marriageable age.

Janie had now become urgently required most evenings. On reaching home from school, she would change into one of her dresses, recently purchased from the latest Littlewood's catalogue. The dress was made of shuntong material, with a little quiver of red and black over a fawn background. It fitted her very well, emphasising her trim, but well built figure.

This evening, she had just missed the bus. There was an hour and a half to wait for the next one. She decided to walk rather than wait all that time. As she was walking about half way up the first hill, a small van drew up. The driver leaned out of the window, "Want a lift?"

"No thank you. Are you going to the top?"

"Yes I am. I'm delivering an order of bread. Are you sure I can't take you there?" She shook her head, feeling just a bit scared. She certainly did not like the look of him. He continued to drive behind her as she walked. "What's the matter, scared are you?" She tried to take no notice of him. She knew, that, a little way up, was a house and people she knew. If she could keep her nerve and reach it without incident, she knew she'd be alright. As she walked and endeavoured to the best of her ability to appear unconcerned, he drove the vehicle in front, blocking her path and stopped. He quickly got out. She succeeded in getting round the rear end and ran as fast as her legs could carry her. He climbed back in and came after her. She reached the gate of the house as soon as he screeched to a halt beside her. She walked backwards up the pathway, her eyes never leaving his face as he walked towards her. She was wishing desperately that someone would come out of the house at that very moment. She tripped as the back of her shoes came in contact with the lower step. Turning, she ran up the steps to the front door and raised her hand to knock. "Go on, knock," he jeered. "I'll get you another time. I'll keep a look out for you, you see if I don't." He climbed back into the van and drove away. It disappeared up the bend of the hill, heading for the village. Again she raised her hand to the knocker. She could hardly breath, she had been so frightened. The sound echoed through the house. There was nobody in. What if he should come back and find her there. Horror filled her. She ran as hard as she could to the hotel, dreading all the while that he would make his appearance again. But at the bottom of the last steep hill she began to feel more secure. She had reached the site of the army tents, where a number of the soldiers who knew her were waving.

Her thoughts were still on the unpleasant event, when feeling hot and sweaty from her enforced exercise, she felt herself in collision with somebody. The papers he was carrying got scattered all over the ground. As they both bent for the purpose of retrieving them, a collision of two heads occurred. Feeling quite dazed, Janie fell back on to her posterior. After a brief pause she looked up into a pair of blue eyes, who's owner was just as dazed and embarrassed as she was. But he was quick to come to her aid and helped her up and offered to get her a drink of water. She did not at first respond to his solicitation, but just continued to stare into his face. She had seen him somewhere before. The flash of his teeth as he smiled set her heart racing.

"Are you alright? Have you far to go?" he was asking.
"No," she replied, "Just to the hotel kitchen."

"Good, I work in the dining room, shall we go there together?" He looked too young to be in uniform, she was thinking.

As they entered the room together, a number of the officers and their staff looked over at them. "So you have met our Janie," said one. The young man turned round to look at her.

"So you're Janie. I've already heard about you." She smiled back at him as she entered the kitchen. No one said a word until the door closed behind her.

In the days that followed, she contrived to hide her feelings concerning the young soldier she had met. One day he happened to give both her and Victoria a lift into the village to do some shopping and to post the mail. He later took them home and he was made welcome. He stayed a short while to meet the rest of the family and partake of a little refreshment. He was quite taken up with Milly, the elder sister, whom he found very amusing. She had her final exams coming up and very much wanted to win the scholarship. Consequently, she was unable to find time to work in the hotel at present.

She had blossomed into a fine looking young woman. He told them that his occupation in the army, more or less matched what he was doing in civilian life. He was sincere in his hopes that nothing would come of this business, as he put it. Having to kill other humans would be terrible. Sometimes he would come in for afternoon tea in the kitchen at the hotel. Janie would sit opposite at the table barely taking her eyes off him. The housemaids would make sly comments. On one occasion, seeing them laughing at her, she made some pretext to leave the room. "You made a conquest there soldier," remarked one wryly.

"I know," said Clive, "Janie would be the sort of girl I should marry if she were older, and of course, if I was not already engaged to be married. I'm to be married in three months time." No time was wasted in transmitting this information to Janie by crueller members of the staff. She was of course stunned by the news. Seeing they were waiting for her reaction, she very haughtily announced that it was of no consequence to her and she found the opportunity, she hastily left the room. That night, Janie cried into her pillow.

As the weeks passed and the pain grew less, Janie, who

could not bring herself to dislike the handsome soldier, pretended all the same to lose interest in him. They still engaged in conversation, passing the time of day and other things, when their meetings were unavoidable. All the same, he did feel a little put out over losing her adoration.

It transpired at about this time, there was a corporal, aged about thirty, who had gained permission to buy and have his meals in the kitchen. He claimed he could not face the food that was dished out to other ranks. It was obvious to everyone that he was a man of some quality and backed by wealth. It was rumoured that his father held a high government position and that he himself was a stockbroker. Be that as it may, he said very little about himself or his affairs. He was the last man to take advantage of his position or connections. During the course of a day, he would unobtrusively make his own observations and enquires. He had found out all about Janie and Clive, and would often notice the sad look on her face when she thought no one was looking at her. He remembered how hurtful the teenage years could be though, now long past nearly forgotten. It happened that one Friday lunchtime, he asked Victoria if she would mind if he took Janie out for a day in London on Saturday. She discussed the matter with Jack, who raised no objection to the proposal, as he had met the man many times, and was very respected by all who knew him. It was therefore arranged that she was to be at the hotel by ten in the morning on the following day.

She was late. Would he still wait for her, she wondered. Would he think she had changed her mind. She slowly climbed the hill. Late as she was, she felt compelled to take in the panoramic view before her. But for the slight mist blurring the horizon, the view would have been much extended. However it gave promise of a perfect day. All the colours of nature seemed to abound at her feet, in the hills that followed one another as they reached the plains below. The heights gave her a feeling of exhilaration. The soldier, unseen, stood watching her. This lovely child unspoilt by time and care. Today would always be remembered by them both. He would forget for a while the finance, war crisis orientated world.

The sun was setting when a car drew up outside the bungalow. Bill, who had been waiting, came out to invite him in for a while. He had to decline the invitation, as he was due back at headquarters. Impulsively, Janie threw her arms around the soldiers neck and kissed him. "Thank you for a really wonderful day. I'll always remember it."

"The pleasure was all mine Janie." She waved until the car was out of sight. She kissed and hugged her father.

"Thanks dad for making this day possible. Thanks for being a smashing dad."
"You must have had a great day in London."

"Yes dad, we simply went everywhere -The Tower; Kew Gardens; Waxworks; Art Galleries and Museums. We even dined of all places, at the Savoy Hotel - it was so posh! Then we finished up at his parents place in Kensington. It's a beautiful house, and they were all so nice to me. It must be good to be rich dad. Just imagine, to be able to buy anything you want!"

"Now, young lady, don't let it turn your head. Being rich isn't everything. Mind you, I'm not against having plenty of money, but it don't always bring the happiness you might expect."
"But a lot of poor people are unhappy too dad,"

commented Janie.

"True my girl, but what you never have, you don't miss," said Bill almost lamely. "Any how young lady, we'd better be going or you'll catch your chill." Janie had time to peep up at the stars. They were smiling down sharing her happiness.

Janie could not help but ponder on the different life between the rich and the poor. Life was such a struggle for those without; which were the many, rather than the few.

She thought about Hammer Go Twice and his desperate situation in life; how a simpleton such as he had battled to keep his family alive; and how it was that the poor rather than the rich came to the aid of these people. Her father was right; money was certainly not everything, she would rather be poor and struggling than lose her humanity and compassion, which was a trait she admired in her father and those around her.

It is amazing what humans can endure and how the human spirit always finds a way to the light. Janie had always had a second sight; she seemed to have an intuition about things and this would be her saving grace for what was yet to come in her life.

Decisions, decisions decisions...

Chapter XLVIII

The headmaster called out for her to enter. Milly pushed the door open peremptorily and entered a small room, she was aware of two well-fed looking men ensconced on either side of him. He greeted her amiably. "Sit down Mildred." They continued to confabulate in low tones among themselves. Once they paused to look at her. Very soon there was a knock at the door and Simon Carter entered. He too was waved into a chair. They all continued murmuring and nodding, looking like a lot of stuffed pigs, with their large paunches and sagging jaws. How she felt she detested them.

At last, one of them spoke as if suddenly aware of their existence, "You also have equal claims to the scholarship, having attained the same number of marks. Unfortunately, we can award it only to one of you. After talking it over, and indeed giving the matter much thought, we think that the practical thing to do would be to hand the scholarship to Simon, after all, he's the one who'll no doubt be the bread winner later on and you Mildred as likely as not will soon get married and settle down to having a family. So Simon, in all justice should be the one selected to further his education, and there the matter must stand."

They were all looking at her. She became aware of the gloating look on the face of her rival, and guessed he must have had prior knowledge of what was going to happen. Flashing indignant eyes around at them, she blurted out, "I supposed the decision arrived at, and, I suppose, already a foregone conclusion, had nothing to do with the fact that Simon Carter is the headmaster's son?" They looked aghast at her cheek. She immediately rose from her chair and without waiting to be dismissed, left the room and went to her classroom. Tears were blinding her. She wiped them away with the back of her hand. In a feeling of rebellion against the system, which favoured the right connections, and male against female, she went to her desk and collecting her personal belongings, she left the school never to return.

Her family were full of sympathy for her. Bill even rang the headmaster, but realised he was up against a solid brick wall of prejudice. What's the best thing for her now, he was thinking. A trade? Why not the tailoring trade? Yes, that's it. Memories of his past years came before him, fighting in the trenches of France, then after, his struggles to get a job and the dole queues - The strikes and hunger marches. The Reynolds family were victims of the depression and in response to this through share desperation, Bill tied a cushion to the bar of his bike, "come on Milly lets earn some cash its pea picking time, we will have food on the table by tea tonight" said Bill. Milly looked into her father's worried face, "is it far to the farms dad?" she asked "yes, but we can make it girl" replied Bill; and so they did.

The soldiers had packed up and left the next day after Janie's trip to London. It seemed the scare was over. But now, the paper boy was shouting, "Paper, paper, read all about it". Apparently, Hitler was at it again. Making fresh demands - War seemed imminent. Dropping the money into the boy's cap lying on the pavement, Bill took one. Perhaps I'll be able to find her a job, he thought.

Milly tears had ceased by the time he reached home. While tea was being prepared, he began to scan the 'situations vacant' column. Only one was advertising for school leavers. Over a million people were unemployed at the time. They read what the prospective employer had to offer – fares paid from destination, stipulating season ticket only, free morning and afternoon tea. Also a hot lunch provided free. She was to learn the trade of tailoring uniforms for railway workers and busmen. Hours of work were from eight o'clock in the morning till five thirty in the evening and a half day on Saturday. On writing to the firm, they were sent a contract to sign, covering a three year agreement. The sum of money that Milly would receive each week would be nine shillings. This would be reviewed every six months if she was keen and applied herself to the job.

    Within a few weeks, Milly and Liz Davenport, who had also applied for the job, accompanied Victoria to the factory, which was situated in Aldgate East, in exceedingly drab surroundings. It was a huge building with stairs to the left and right of it, leading to floors on either side. They were guided by a young girl to the second floor on the right. They were approached by a grey haired elderly man known as Mr George. Victoria introduced the two girls to him. He then began to show them round. There were long benches supporting numerous machines worked by girls of various ages under twenty. All eyes appeared to fasten on them as they walked round. They turned their heads to murmur among themselves and those opposite. All were anxious to find out what they could about the newcomers. But this could not last, as conveyor belts, a recent innovation to speed up production and keep idle chatter to a minimum, with pieces of garment in various stages of manufacture, kept them almost ceaselessly at their tasks. If anyone lagged behind, the faster ones invariably came to their aid, for despite the conditions of slavery, that wonderful spirit of the East End Londoner was always there and which would exemplify itself later on in the blitz.

 Older and more experienced machinists sewed the canvas and striped material to the inside waste band in readiness for the buttons and bar-tracking machines and pressers. Other sections did waistcoats and jackets for the railway and bus uniforms. Overcoats and ladies costumes were manufactured on other floors. Bespoke tailoring was carried out by specialists who were usually male Jews. Mrs Denam was then introduced. She showed them to the cloakroom and toilets. After wishing them goodbye Victoria was relieved to be able to leave the building. Victoria over the years was used to such places. But those conveyor belts were another story. She did not like the look of them – no, not one bit.

Milly and Liz were bewildered by all the noise and hubbub and the many strange looking people they were so suddenly thrown amongst. It was like bedlam to say the least. What in heaven's name were they doing here? Was the constant voice of Milly thoughts. At lunch and tea breaks they clung together as if their lives depended on it. They would follow the crowd up what seemed to be endless flights of stairs to the massive room at the top, which was the canteen. A huge woman superintended over numerous assistants, as they rushed to serve the queues of people in time, before the bell rang to resume work again.

Feeling tired and complaining of headaches, both girls joined the rush to the clocking machines. They drew the cards from the rack, showing their numbers and names and clocked out. They welcomed the short walk to the station after sitting on hard seats all day. When they reached the station, they lost sight of one another in the crowd for a short time. However, Liz called from the carriage she had boarded on spotting Milly. Both were thankful to be on their why home again. "What a long and exhausting day it has been," said Milly. Liz agreed.

Chapter XLIX

Within a week the girls were beginning to settle in. Milly became popular with her peers but Liz was slower to make friends being a more reserved girl. When pay day arrived, once a week, they would finger their pay packets with excitement and satisfaction. Leaving them unopened, they would place them in their handbags. At home they would compare their earnings with what they picked up at the hotel and considered it a pittance. "You can't bank on the hotel, that could finish for us any day," Bill would wisely proclaim.

After dinner, while the family were still sitting, she would proudly tip the eight shillings on to the table (a shilling had been stopped for reasons they could never fathom). It had been decided to deduct five shillings, from her pay for board, leaving her with three shillings spending money. Bill would reiterate that time worn phrase of his, "Remember, the thing to keep in mind, it's a trade and you'll always have it to fall back on."

Bill had no realisation of how long he had been waiting when he became suddenly aware of Ben speaking to him from behind. "No sign of her?" Both stood still on the platform, even though the train had already departed some minutes ago, one would have thought that they expected another train to follow any minute. Ben turned towards the station telephone. "If you can give me a description of what she was wearing today, I'll phone along the lines. Someone might have seen her." But after spending sometime on the phone, he drew a blank. No one, it appeared, had seen Milly.

Halfpenny whinnied, snorted and pawed the ground. Ben observed him vacantly, "Can smell the storm, animals can." The last few words were lost in a violent clap of thunder, causing the animal to rear in fright. Huge drops of rain were heard beating on the tin roof. Untying the reins, and speaking softly to quieten him, Milly climbed into the trap and headed for home. Perhaps she might already be at home, perhaps she's been given a lift thought Bill hopefully. Lightning snaked its way across the sky, illuminating the hills. Already he was being drenched by the rain. The light streamed a welcome from the door when he reached Bognor Regis, but the warm fire inside did not hold its usual appeal, his mind was too troubled.

Victoria had been listening for the trap. She stood in the doorway waiting for Milly to alight. She looked troubled when she saw that he was alone. "What on earth could have happened to her," exclaimed Bill. "Ben phoned through for me at the station and there hasn't been a sign of her." Janie was lying awake in her bedroom. She shared the room with her sister in front of the house. She could hear every word that was spoken. Milly not back! Where could she be?

Housing Halfpenny in his stall and feeding him, Bill looked for a while to see if Rose's kennel had remained dry inside. The kennel, he discovered, was dry, but there was no sign of Rose. Probably slipped her collar again, he thought. She'll soon be back on a night like this. Going into the washhouse, he quickly slipped out of his wet clothes and donned dry ones. But going to bed was out of the question. He took Janie in a cup of warm cocoa. "Come on my girl, time you were asleep." He hesitated as if about to ask her something, but then changed his mind. "Get some sleep girl," he said instead.

When he left the room, she lay there with no thought in her head of going to sleep. Her door had been left open and the hall light was streaming into her bedroom. She could see by the clock on the dresser that it was two thirty in the morning. Her father's footsteps sounded in the hall. Victoria was asking him to button up his mac. "If the police station is closed, I'll knock him up at his house," he was saying.

Halfpenny was harnessed once again. As he set off down the lane the thunder could still be heard, but some distance away now, although it was still raining quite heavily. Janie, could not bear the tension any longer. Throwing the bed covers back, she got out of bed and slipping into her slippers, she quickly donned her dressing gown and made her way into the kitchen to join her mother. She sat in dad's chair and observing Victoria looking so distraught, endeavoured to cheer her up. "She'll be alright mum, don't you worry," she reassured her.

The blue lamp outside the police station was easy to see, even in the rain. Bill rang the bell, but getting no reply he headed towards the residence. The door was answered by a short stout little woman, who he took to be Mrs Piper. "He's just been called out," she said when she saw Jack. "Is it anything serious?" she asked when she saw how troubled he looked.

"It's my daughter. She hasn't arrived home from work. I'm very worried, as this sort of thing has never happened before." She was very sympathetic.

"I don't know how long he'll be, but I'll give him your message."

"Thanks mam," replied Bill. He did not go immediately home, but drove round to the station, entertaining the forlorn hope that she could perhaps have been waiting there. Then he drove round for about another hour, unable to face going home just yet. When he did finally come home, it was already four in the morning. Victoria looked up at him as he walked in. She had been filling in her time on making a rag mat which she had only just completed. He was dripping wet, and he stood spilling rain water all over it. She did not appear to notice this in her anxiety for any news he could give her. A loud knocking sounded on the door startling them. It was policeman Piper, he had another policeman with him.

"May we come in?" Bill let them in sensing that something was very wrong. They were offered a warm drink which they accepted. They warmed their hands by the fire, as Bill looked expectantly at them. "You left a description of your daughter with my wife," said Constable Piper to Bill. The latter nodded, not finding the voice to speak. "We have a description here of a young girl that nearly matches the one you gave." Her body was found in a deserted building some four miles from here. We suspect murder. Victoria cried out and Bill put his arm round her. Janie felt she wanted to be sick.

"Not Milly. This can't happen to us. Our Milly, always so full of life."

"It's a long way to go, mind you, we can't be certain at this stage. It could well prove to be somebody else. We thought, after much heart searching on my part, that we might as well put you in the picture now rather than later on, if it should happen to be your daughter - if you'll let me have a photograph meantime." He was speaking to Bill but eyeing Victoria as he spoke. She looked at the large photographs in their frames on the mantelpiece. One picture was of Janie and the other of Milly. She took Milly's down and handed it over. She was feeling numb inside. She felt she was just having a bad dream, and would soon wake up. They took the photograph and left, assuring them that they would be back very soon, hopefully with good news.

Bill walked out presently saying that he could do with some fresh air. His hands shook as he tried to light a cigarette. He threw it away with an impatient gesture and walked round to the back of the house. He stumbled over an object in the dark. Bending over to feel it, his hands came into contact with something warm and sticky. He quickly ran into the house to see what was on his hands, to discover they were covered in blood. "The torch!" he shouted, "Where is the torch?" Janie brought it to him. She was horrified at the sight of blood. "Stay in," he ordered her. On returning, he shone the torch and discovered Rose lying in a pool of blood. Bringing the light closer, he gently examined her. A bullet had gone through her neck, just missing her windpipe. She was in a mess, but still alive. Wasting no time, he quickly got her to the local vet, who was averse to being woken up at such an early hour. However, on seeing the critical condition of the dog, he had her carried straight away to the surgery, where he was to operate on her. Jack excused himself, informing the surgeon he had trouble, but would be back very soon.

He had to comfort Janie on returning. She could take no more of this terrible night. Rose will live, he assured her. Even though she was badly wounded, she was tough and would pull through, of that he was certain. Bill ordered her to bed. He waited up until about the time when he thought that Milly would be due to start work at the factory, and drove to the phone box. He waited impatiently for the girl at the other end to locate her, if she were in. After what he considered an eternity of time, he heard her voice at the other end. He was too overcome with relief to answer back for a while. "Is that you dad?" she was saying. "Hello dad, are you alright?" He managed to speak at last,

"Yes, I'm alright dear, we have all been so worried at home that you didn't come back. What happened?"

"Oh, I'm sorry dad, you know that girl Ester Woodward? Well she's getting married on Saturday. We had a bit of a celebration at work and afterwards I had to help her carry her presents home. I missed the last train home."

"That's alright dear."

"Dad if Liz Davenport had been in work she would have told you but she was home sick yesterday." After putting the phone down, Jack was surprised that he hadn't flown off the handle after the night's ordeal. He was just relieved to hear her voice, she was alive and well.

Constable Piper was waiting for him. He could tell from Bill's face all was well. "I'm glad," he said, returning the photograph. "We have discovered the identity of the other poor girl and the description of a man seen about the time in the area. You're probably had all can take for one night. Good day to you."

John Davenport had left school and was now working in a garage, where he could tinker with cars to his heart's content. Today he was out testing one, when he described Janie entering the sweet shop next to the school. He stopped the car, and crossing the road, entered the shop. She had just ordered her banana split milk toffee, and the man behind the counter was at that moment breaking it into small pieces for her with a toffee hammer. Weighing a pennyworth, he handed it over to her. John, who had been standing behind her, stretched out his hand and paid the shopkeeper the penny. She turned in surprise and a little confusion, to see his smiling good-natured face. "Thanks John," she said.

"Can I give you a lift home Janie?" he asked. She nodded, her mouth being full of toffee. Crossing the road, they climbed into the Bentley sports car belonging to Mr Lansbury, the hotel proprietor. "How about a little ride round first Janie?" She nodded, still chewing her toffee. She took off her velour school hat and her golden hair flowed in the breeze as they set off. He drove the car well. It just purred under his touch. Silence was maintained, she began to praise him. It must have been what he was waiting for. "I'm set on getting my own business Janie. I'll do up old cars and sell them. One can get a lot of money that way. You just see, in a few years, I'll get enough together to start off on my own. There's only the garage I work for. He charges too much. He could sure do with a bit of competition." Janie looked admiringly at him,

"You know what you want out of life John?" He stopped the car in a quite narrow road and said,
" I sure do Janie." He bent over and kissed her. She was surprised, annoyed, but very delighted all the same. She said coyly,

"You shouldn't have done that John."

"But I've wanted to do that for a long time Janie," he said quietly. "Am I forgiven?"
"You're forgiven," she said. They were both laughing. Within a few minutes he had dropped her outside her gate at Bognor Regis. Victoria recognised the sports car as it drew up outside the house. A message had been sent to her from the

hotel to report immediately. John offered to drop her there, as he had to return the car. Janie quickly got out so as to be at home when her brothers returned from school.

When Victoria reached the Hotel, Mr Grant informed her that Mr Lansbury was waiting to see her. She was to go to his office immediately. He was standing at the window looking out. "Close the door Victoria." He was looking worried. "Christ, the way things are going, we could soon be at war. The man's a lunatic. Did you hear him on the radio the other night Victoria? Oh damn!" Something else more private was troubling him beside the international situation she thought. He seemed to have come to some sort of decision, for within a little while, he drew himself to his full height and turned round to face her. "Victoria," he was saying, "I know I can trust you, so I'll tell you what has happened. My wife has finally left me for that officer Newton, who was here with the army." He continued for a while as if lost in thought. "I would like yourself and Jack to manage the hotel for me until it is sold." She felt a bit worried about this, how would the staff react she wondered, especially Mr Grant. As if knowing what was troubling her, he said, "Don't worry, Victoria, I shall arrange for a staff meeting very shortly. I want the matter thrashed out before I take my leave tonight."

He was as good as his word. At the meeting he informed the staff of his intentions - he was going to let Victoria and Jack take over the running of the hotel. Happily there was no distension to his proposal, saying that he would be away for a few months and hoped sincerely that they would cooperate with the new management. He left the hotel, followed by Mr Grant, who perhaps would have known more than the others, except Victoria, about the situation. They walked to where the car had been left. He locked the boot after placing the suitcases in it, he handed the hotel keys to Mr Grant to pass on to Victoria, he whistled in the direction of the yard. Two brown forms appeared at his feet in the twilight gloom, they quickly jumped into their places in the car at his command. The two men shook hands. "Goodbye Mr Grant, it's been a pleasure knowing you."

"Goodbye Sir, the very best of luck to you." The former, it was told, ended his life at Dunkirk. True or fable? And Mr Grant? All contact was lost. The red sports car was soon extinguished by the darkness of the impending night.

Chapter L

Bill was very much opposed to the idea of running the hotel as it would entail living on the premises. At first they looked to making daily trips there but the impracticably of the situation forced on them the need to eventually move into the premises. They were waiting for the transport to convey their luggage to the hotel. Most of them were quite excited at the prospect and liked the idea of living on top of a hill in luxurious surroundings. "How long do we have to wait for the lorry dad?" asked Milly. Bill paused before answering,

"I'd say about another hour, we're quite early."
"Can me and Janie take Rose for a walk?"

"Alright, but don't be too long about it." Except for the neck, which had been close cropped for the operation, no one could have believed that Rose had very nearly died from a gunshot. She was now as strong as ever. The girls had a light horse chain attached to her collar, yet they were still afraid she might break it. They headed towards the cinder track, but Janie stopped, "I don't feel like walking down that lonely path it's creepy, I feel something bad could happen to us if we do"

"Don't be daft sis, replied Milly". We have been down it many times, and I need to collect the new timetable, at the station." They had been walking for about a quarter of an hour enjoying the crispness of the early morning air and the scent of the late spring flowers when Rose suddenly stopped straining at the leash and became still. Impatiently, the girls started to tug at her, reluctantly, it seemed, she began to walk with them again. They had only moved a few yards when she stopped again. The hair on her back could be visibly seen to rise and she barred her teeth and growled. They looked in the direction in which she was growling. Standing a short distance away was a well dressed young man, wearing an open mac over his suit and a trilby hat on his head. On seeing himself the centre of attention from both the dog and girls, he lowered his hat over his face and moved away deeper into the woods. This excited Rose to a frenzy. She tugged at the chain so hard that the girls were forced to let go of it. She ran after the man taking the chain with her. The man now began to run. Rose was forced to gyrate in her efforts to negotiate the trees, having looped herself around a tree. On seeing this, he immediately became emboldened, and began to walk towards the girls. They knew he meant to harm them, and began to judge their chances of freeing the half frenzied dog in time. They made vain attempts at undoing the collar, but the vigorous movements of the animal prevented this. They still continued with their efforts to free her, but he was almost upon them. He had already reached them, when by some quirk of fate, the dog managed to free herself. He pulled out a gun from his coat pocket. The sight maddened the dog. She leapt at him regardless of danger to herself The girls ran, as a shot rang out, down the cinder track they went on until they reached the steps which took them up into the station. The man behind the counter of the newspaper shop at their behest phoned the police.

On reaching the place where the encounter had taken place, the police had no difficulty in arresting the man, for they found he had been pinned down by the dog and was unable to move. She had her teeth bared just a fraction from his throat, he dare not move an inch as she would have ripped at neck. He was eventually charged and tried for the murder of a local girl. "That's the person who must have shot Rose. She must have tried to protect the girl that night," Bill said. The lorry had since arrived and had been waiting a long time. "We must get a move on," insisted Bill. "Mr Grant is to have a meal waiting for us."

"Do you mean that we ourselves will be waited on," said Milly.
"Mr Grant will have it no other way. Mrs Davenport is now the cook."

"It'll be funny working in a factory all day and come home to be waited on, and all that luxury too." Bill sighed impatiently,

"I sure hope they will hurry up and sell the place, so we can all go back to normal living again." But George, who loved food, thought about the many visits he could make to the fridge to help himself to jelly and ice cream.

They were surprised that the hotel was to run so smoothly. Victoria suspected the great influence of Mr Grant who commanded great respect from the staff. He was a just, kind and generous man, who never went near a church. One would say that he was inbred with the Christian spirit rather than the letter.

The family enjoyed the novelty of being waited on. Mr Grant would insist that they were now his employers. Bill took charge of the bar, and as there was little outside work for him to do, he was able to give it his undivided attention. His sister, Mrs Felton, who had already been down to visit them a few times, decided that she would come down every weekend to help out, Victoria got her the job of collecting money and issuing tickets for the weekly dance. She also took care of the cloakrooms. The money she earned was put away for special occasions. Bill liked having his sister visiting, and they were to learn what a kind person she was.

One day, however, a crisis was to arise. One of the stewards was seen making clandestine visits to one of the housemaids bedrooms. He was tackled one morning by the head steward and given notice of dismissal. The maid was sent for by Victoria, and the latter broke down weeping saying that she had been secretly engaged to the man for six months and she was now nearly three months pregnant. She did not want to work another nine months pregnant; for a woman was not allowed to work once she was married. She did want to work another month longer if this could be arranged. After conferring with Mr Grant on the plight of the couple, the steward was immediately reinstated, and the maid allowed too stay for as long as she could manage to work. The wedding date was set and a reception arranged, all the staff assisted with donations.

Time passed, the leaves were young and fresh on the trees. One day an elderly couple walked in and announced that they were the new owners. The Reynolds moved back to their bungalow and Victoria decided to stay at home for a while to have a well earned rest. The situation in Europe was on the boil again after Chamberlain's attempt at appeasement. Janie was sitting for her exams later in the year. They did not expect the high results from her that Milly had achieved. This was, after all immaterial to what her parents had already planned for her. For whether she liked it or not, she was to join her illustrious sister in the factory at Aldgate East, the perpetual enlistment to society's slavery, unconsciously perpetuated by the innocent, at the silent behest of the rulers. Janie at first argued the point. She said she would like to be in the fashion world or even a dress maker. She had enough foresight to realise at her young age, the despair of the human soul engaged in factory occupations. The enlightened surely did not engage in such labours. She even preferred hotel work. "What," thundered her father, "Wait on people all your life, never. A trade will always guarantee you work. Clothes surely would always be in demand." The subject was irrevocably closed.

    Milly had gone to a dance in London with Lizzie Davenport and a few other friends. She had informed Bill that she would be back on the last train. He met the train, but there was no sign of either girl. This caused him to fume and fret after remembering the last experience. Victoria suggested they wait up until two the morning. "It's a comfort to know that at least she's with friends," she said. But it was three o'clock, when standing on the steps of the porch, he described her coming down the lane. She entered the gate, and laughed nervously when she saw him waiting. He did not call out his usual greeting to her, this was a bad sign, and she knew she must expect the worst. Imperviously she approached the front door. In his anger he began to raise his hand as if to strike her a blow. Ducking under it, she quickly darted into the hall. She caught her shoe in the last step and left it behind. In her effort to move forward, she collided with the door and dropped her handbag. On reaching the bedroom, she quickly locked herself in. Victoria reached the scene, be-searching him to calm down and come into the kitchen. "It'd be better to talk it over in the morning," she suggested. Bill reluctantly followed her advice.

There followed a period of silence while she prepared a drink. She could see, however, that he was dwelling on the matter. "I've been thinking," he said at last. He swallowed the remainder of his tea. "I've been turning the matter over for a few weeks now. Ted is now fully recovered from his illness, there's no complaints regarding the youngest." Victoria sniffed,

"I know," she said, "you want to move back to London again."
He looked at her quizzically,
"You've guessed right girl. Alright with you is it?" There was a moment of silence before she spoke.

"I love this place and will be sorry to leave it. But if it's in the interest of the family to move back, well of course I'm all for it."

"The girls are growing up now," said Jack. "They must want the benefits of city life, besides; they spend many hours travelling to get anywhere. Also our Janie will be starting work soon."

And so the germ of the idea took root and began to germinate and flourish. Milly duly apologised the following morning. The family then met to discuss Bill's proposal of returning to London. After much opposition and tears from the children, a final decision in favour of returning was reached, although the thought of leaving 'Laindon Hills' after having made it their home town for so many years seemed both monstrous and impossible.

The advent of Janie's exams and their outcome were given hardly any consideration by her parents. Had she been a genius, it would have made very little difference to the outcome. It was ruled, 'what was good enough for her sister, was good enough for her.' So in due course of time, poor Janie was to find herself travelling to work with a group of girls, with whom she toiled on the same floor. It was a little easier for her to settle in, as her sister Milly was able to help her in many ways. However, her proud way of carrying herself, soon came to be resented by many. They regarded her as being 'stuck up.' Mr George had started her on pairing the legs of trousers. She found this difficult at first, as she had to keep up with the work coming off the conveyor belts, particularly as the matching numbers were invariably all mixed up. She was to suffer from the heat, as the table at which she worked was close to the steam pressers. The women who worked them never spoke a word all day. They were indeed true zombies. One of the 'mute' women, she noticed, was small and wiry, with sharp bird like eyes. Her hair was plaited into a large bun at the back of her head. Her mode of dress was extremely formal. One got the impression from closer scrutiny, of just two pieces of material sewn together. When she had to leave her work bench, she would as if balancing on roller skates, her arms flung out and legs splayed as if to prevent herself from falling over. "Be careful not to draw her attention to you," the girls warned her. "She is likely to round on you, and cause you a lot of embarrassment."

"Why is she like it?" Janie asked.

"She's an old maid; she has been working here for years – part of the furniture, so to speak. It's said she lost her sweetheart during the last war. She turned batty and has remained batty ever since."

It was often difficult to hold conversations above the noise of the machines. As the days went by, it became evident how little importance they could exchange in conversation, during their short breaks, such was the effect of the factory upon them. They would often take to singing however. By this means, they would feel elevated above the meanness of their surroundings. They would all join in the singing. Most of them were cockneys coming from the surrounding districts of Stepney Green, Rotherhithe and Aldgate. Janie, when she listened would liken them to birds singing in a cage. She herself would often join in the singing. A little Jew man, superbly dressed, short and round, like the world globe, would sometimes stand there, wearing a pleased expression. When they finished he would amble away. "The boss," one of the girls whispered in Janie's ear. "Bloody Jew!" said another.

Whatever plans the girls had for the weekend were to be rudely shattered, for Bill announced suddenly that they would be moving back to London the following Saturday. All their help would be enlisted for packing. They remonstrated, "What about Halfpenny, the chickens, the goats, the rabbits..." which had multiplied, "...the two cats and Rose?"

"Don't worry your heads," exclaimed Bill. "They will all be given to the Davenports, they had taken care of them all while we were living in the hotel. Rose of course, would go with them to London."

"What about Halfpenny?" Bill looked downcast as he told them that he had already been sold and would be collected by his new master on Saturday.

It was a sad business for the Reynolds family. To be severed from a mode of life they had become accustomed to. They had been very happy, and now this. It would mean no more fresh eggs and honey, apples and plums picked straight from the tree; homemade bread and jam. No more gathering wild flowers in the woods in springtime and picking mushrooms the size of dinner plates on misty September mornings - calls of the cuckoo on warm spring days, the lowing of herds coming in from the pastures to be milked. They would no longer hear the cry of the owl and the nightingale, which had so often perched on the parlour window ledge to trade its heavenly warble, so it seemed for a few crumbs of bread. No more chasing with Rose across the paddocks and swinging on the swings. Janie felt a deep anguish within her breast.

On Friday evening, the Davenports, Upjohn's and many other friends, joined them in a farewell get together. Mr Grant and a few of the staff from the hotel also managed to attend. They all spoke together of old times. 'Do you remember...' was an opening phrase in common usage that evening. It had its sadder moments they all agreed, but anyway, that was life wasn't it? One had to accept the rough with the smooth. John Davenport singled Janie out and asked her to walk with him for the last time over their old haunts. "Tomorrow, Janie we'll sit on the swings and remember what it used to be, just as the grown-ups are doing – what you say?" With tears in her eyes, she looked at him and nodded approval.

John called at eight the following morning, in company with his sisters and brothers. Milly, Janie, Ted, George, Brenda and Egan were all ready to set out as planned. Victoria watched them from the window. She mused, the last time they will walk the lanes and fields together. What did the future hold for them? She pondered.

They all followed the well beaten track which led through Farmer Harrison's Farm, passing the place where the cattle had taken to Sid that day and the pond he had fallen into. They could afford to laugh about it now. They swung for a while on the swings and whisked madly on the roundabouts and bumped each other on the see-saws. After, they began to chase each other. Janie, at one stage, was chased by John, as she ran, she fell. Her hands came into contact with the blackened grass left by the round house and the strange men. She was to learn one day, what all this meant, but for the present, she was content not to worry herself about the incident. "Oh Janie, come on! You're such a day dreamer," remonstrated John. He helped her to her feet. They were both overcome by sadness. "It's time we got back," he said.

"We'll write to each other," said Janie, "We'll come over and see you sometimes." He shook his head.

"Janie deep within me, I feel we shall never see each other again - events which followed were to prove him correct. (John joined the army to deal as a mechanic as was in charge of the lorries. His friend had driven a lorry up towards where John was standing against a wall; but he left the truck in gear and it ran down the slope and crushed John against the wall)Taking one of her hands with the palm facing upwards, he kissed it, and closed her fingers over it to symbolise its eternal retention. She in turn, blew him a kiss, and with tears streaming down her cheeks, ran for home. No one could catch up with her. She seemed to go with the wind, her golden hair flowing like a cloud behind her.

Victoria had some refreshments waiting. The lorry was

already waiting at the gate. Halfpenny had just been harnessed by his new master and the children hugged and kissed him goodbye. It was like saying goodbye to childhood. It was so for the two girls. Ted and George still had a few years ahead of them.

All too soon, they were in the lorry with Rose and the goldfish. Uncle Max, Aunt Grace, Brenda and Egan, the Davenports and Upjohn's, were all standing under the large lime tree in the front of 'Bognor Regis.' That dear little house, that had within it so many happy memories. It looked beautiful and well cared for, with its rose gardens and trim lawns. The final goodbyes were exchanged. The storekeeper and his wife rushed out to get their farewells in. The lorry rumbled away with its load of humanity and chattels on the road of life and the way was winding.

Chapter LI

London

A year had passed since the Reynolds family had returned. A million or more unemployed! Times were hard. The North of England had been in hard times much longer, so many were looking for jobs in the South. So queues grew longer and longer. A few hours or a whole days work was thankfully received. It put bread on the table, for handouts at the dole office were pitifully small.

Bill had joined the union and was trying to get work as a 'ship wielder' for he had done such work before. He had been working for the last week at the shipyards, loading barley sacks on to a ship. A job even the most desperate was reluctant to participate in - now Bill had learnt why. For at this moment, Victoria was cutting his shirt off piece by piece. The barley, had pierced his skin in dozens of places, leaving large scratches in their wake and blood had oozed and dried hard. The pain must have been terrible, for it was horrible to look at. Gently she bathed bits of shirt off his back, to prevent the skin coming away with it, leaving the raw flesh exposed. "They finished me off today," said Bill.

"In more ways than one," retorted an angry Victoria. "It'll take weeks to heal, and you'll not be able to sleep on your back without pain anyway."

It was August, the year 1939 – a really wonderful summer! Most of the younger family members and older ones, who still loved camping, had joined their friends at the train station; others had taken their car and tents. "See you down there," they shouted as they headed towards 'Frittenden', a quaint little village in 'the garden of England' as Kent was called. A lot of the campers, 'old timers', had been coming down for years. Hop picking brought got them a holiday and friends – both among the Londoners and locals. (This was an annual event, all the holiday-makers would rise early in the morning mist and make their way to the hop fields; where hundreds of hop vines hung. A man would pull the vines down and take them to the bins where whole families would stand picking the hops and singing at the top of their voices – these people were mostly Londoners from the East End; it brought in extra cash for Christmas)

Still singing, arm in arm, they went down the lane, after the pub had closed, then round the camp fires, where tall tales were told. The locals were not short of telling a few themselves.

Vincent, the son of a policeman, home from college, was showing great interest in Milly, who had blossomed into a lovely young woman. But this was cut short by Arthur, who arrived at the weekend, for he and Milly had become engaged. He had just completed his apprenticeship as tugboat master, bringing in the big liners. His father was a captain in the navy, so the sea was in their blood. Vincent was not to be out done, for there were many pretty girls to choose from, as he was a handsome lad. So many friends had joined them by the second week, but there was plenty of room, and plenty of food, for everyone had put money towards it, making it a very cheap and enjoyable holiday. The children had gone everywhere; even in the local pub there was a room for them to play, drink lemonade, have crisps and sweets. Ted and George said they loved it. It reminded them of Laindon Hills and they wished they were back there. "Can't turn the clock back boys," said Bill.

'War' was declared on September 3rd 1939. Chamberlain, the Prime Minister of England, had given Hitler three days to get out of Poland. Hitler thumbed his nose at him and England was at war. Upheaval, was in every household. Children were to be sent into the country. Young men, called up or signed up. Panic and tears filled the air for the safety of their loved ones. Some found it exciting. Money was found for war, if not peace and unemployment came to an all time low.

"Read all about it, read all about it," shouted the ragged paper boy in the street. "Chamberlain out, Churchill in." A sigh of relief ran through the nation.

"Thank goodness it's Churchill, not Lord Halifax. For one is a winner the other a loser," said Bill (who was now working on the ships). But Dunkirk was just around the corner, the horror of it not revealed to those up high, but had already hit the man in the streets. Many feared for their loved ones.

Janie answered the door, "Blackout," shouted the warden. "Want to be killed do you? Your light is showing upstairs. Why aren't you in your dugout?"

"Sorry Uncle Max," she said, for he was now head warden, having moved to London six months ago. Brenda had also joined the A.R.P. The blitz, found her at one time sitting on a 500lb bomb ready to go off any moment! While Uncle Max and others were moving the soil around a trapped woman, Brenda was calming her down. "They didn't tell me," she said afterwards. "I'd have ran a mile if I'd have known," which made her listeners smile for she was always in trouble.

A long-time friend of the family, Vincent was standing at the door, when Victoria opened it. He had been many times to the Reynolds family abodes for they had been bombed out so many times it was hard to keep up with them. Milly had married Arthur, when he was called up in the army – not navy? He had been posted to Scotland and wanted her with him. The Reynolds family was down to Bill, Victoria, Janie and Rose. But soon Janie would be on the move. In the meantime, Vincent, now in the air force, had spent some of his leaves in the past year in London with Janie and her friends who were few and far between these days as most of them were in some government service. However, Billy Lane, who was an officer in the air force, would bring a friend and the four of them would attend a Saturday night dance at one of the camps they were stationed at. But this leave was Vincent's last, for he was in transit, which meant in his case, overseas. "Where do you think they will send you?" Janie asked, when they were alone.

"My guess is India." Bill and Victoria were sad to see him go. Victoria's brothers were in the Royal Marines and were in many battles on the high seas, some famous ones. It was midnight, but Janie insisted on walking to the station with him. Pitch black and bombed out streets greeted them. A "sad" London indeed. "How's Ted and George going in the country?" he asked.

"Not good at the moment. The farmer makes them work hard after school and they want to come home."

"Not wise," said Vincent. The station in sight, both hurried for this was the last train. It came hooting, blowing steam and coal dust everywhere. "Take care of yourself Janie. I don't know if we will meet again."

"Don't be silly, of course we will," she said. The train was pulling out of the station when he leant out of the carriage window and shouted,

"Wait for me Janie." Yes I will! shouted Janie after him. Her affirmation was akin to being engaged with Vincent. His next four years were spent in India and Burma.

Janie felt lost without her sister and brothers. She spent many nights reading. She had a leather bound book of all 'Sherlock Homes" stories. Wordsworth was her favourite poet. A book she kept for many years and read time and time again. The Battle of Britain, kept one on their toes just watching and shouting as they fought in the sky above them. "Give it to them," Bill would shout. He had tried to join up, but like Janie, his work at the shipyard was regarded as important. He had gone through the worst bombing ever of the docks, still working on the ships knowing how desperate England was for shipping. He was not alone, for England was for the English! Not bloody Hitler and his henchmen. "You'll see girl," he would say, so tired he could hardly keep his eyes open.

Arthur and Milly were back in London after their stay in Scotland. He too, was on embarkation leave. They were expecting their first child. He was to spend many years away, one of the 'desert rats'. Many of his army pals came during his last leave. What great fun they were. One of them however, proved to be a thorn in Janie's side (so to speak). Alan had just been demobilised, meaning discharged through medical grounds, though to look at him, one would not have seen it. 'Waterworks' someone whispered into Janie's ear.

He would be sitting on the old rocking chair waiting for her to come home from work. Always immaculately dressed, he was the son of a rich merchant, who was used to getting his own way. Janie took her meals in the kitchen, "What can I do about him Mum? He said he won't give up until I promise to go out with him."

"There has been a lull in the bombing and you haven't been out anywhere, except work." So Janie promised this coming Saturday they would go out together. That kept him away for the rest of the week.

After working Saturday morning, she thought it would be nice to buy a dress. The girls at work told her she could buy one for less coupons if she paid more at certain dress shops. Due to the lull in bombing, stalls were being put out in the market place. Having just purchased a red dress that had made a hole in her pay packet, Janie saw two soldiers approach a man putting handbags onto a stall. He tried to make a run back into the shop. They waylaid him. The girls at work had spoken of the men holed up, "No ration books, no I.D. Cards. So can't be called up, the bloody cowards! but making plenty down the markets." Now one was holed up so to speak.

"Why aren't you in uniform?" questioned one of the soldiers.
"None of your business," was the answer.

"Well I'm bloody well making it my business. We lost a lot of our mates at Dunkirk and the likes of you lot get off scot-free."

"Living off the fat of the land," said the other solider. Janie thought she would like a little of that fat back, having paid such a high price for the dress. More men came from the shops to back him up. This seemed to please the soldiers. The more the merrier they thought. "You bloody cowards! said the soldier, who had by now worked his way into a certain position.

"Well it's like this," said one of the men, "Your King, our country." replied the Stall holder. That did it – up went the stalls, the fish barrels made everything slimy, clothes, the lot, it was full on. Two policemen appeared.
"ello, ello, what's going on here?" as if they didn't know. The soldiers were brushing themselves down and the men had rushed back to their holes.
"I'm just getting a few things straightened sir." The policemen smiled. Janie continued on her way home to face the man in the rocking chair and there he was!

"We'll be going to the West End, dine at the Savoy hotel and I want to buy you something." said Alan, Janie groaned. Why didn't she like him? It was hard to tell. He was good looking, well mannered, plenty of money. It was his arrogance that was it. And she was to spend a whole evening with him. Poor Janie, what lay ahead was far, far worse.

They had just left Charring Cross underground station, and were walking up the steep hill, when the 'warning' sounded. Having just reached the top, when a pulsating noise brought fear into their hearts. They had heard that sound many times. "Here's the main station, let's wait in there," he said.

"They go for stations," said Janie

"We have no choice." The pulsating drone was above. "Christ there's hundreds of the buggers." They dashed for cover. So it seemed, there were hundreds more, as the huge station began to fill up. The whine of the bombs could be heard, for despite the large numbers of people, all were silent, broken only by new comers.

"The docks are getting it again," someone said. "Poor buggers." Her dad was there, also many people worked and lived close by in Silver Town (what a name for such a place). But they had to stay put. Why? Money of course – who could live without it? Yet, in war, it could make the difference between life or death. Whole factories had moved to the countryside to keep produce going. A bomb fell close by, shaking the station.

"That was a close one," someone remarked.
"Well there's plenty coming down." Alan touched Janie's arm,

"I'll get some tea, do you want something to eat?" she shook her head, looking around the station it was full of uniformed people – men and women. I must get out and do my bit. She mused, A.R.P for a few hours after work (Air Raid Precautions) on two nights a week. She wore the Red Cross band around her arm, when the alarm sounded at work, was last to leave the floor. Not good enough , she thought. Alan came back with the tea. "Sorry about this Janie"

"Not your fault and thank you for the tea Alan." The 'all clear' sounded. "We had better return home," said Janie. They were on their way down the hill to Charring Cross underground station, when the warning sounded again. The pulsating drone seemed louder and heavier than before.

"Run back to the station Janie. I'll see if the trains are running underground," said Alan. When he returned, he remarked, "It's all out slaughter out there, the East End is up in flames, no trains, stations hit, no buses as yet, we're stuck here." People screamed as bombs fell near.

"They're going for the station," said Janie.
"It's all out bombing tonight," replied Alan. And he was right.

One had to be careful, very careful, for there were holes in the roads, on the pavements. All were black shadows against a brilliant orange-red sky. It was London – burning, bombed, crying out for help, but few would listen. "They're done for," the American Ambassador had said as he flew back home after the fall of France. So Britain and the British fought on alone against the might of Hitler. Where ever he sent his troops, ours were there also.

Getting home was Janie's worry. No, or very few buses (all full of course). Some trains still running, but not in her direction. People digging in the rubble of bombed buildings, risking their own lives should the walls above collapse. Gas mains broken; water pipes broken – no water to fight the flames, no lights to look deep into the darkest corners, walking shadows everywhere. Still we fought on, we had Churchill and he had us!

"Alan, we have reached Forrest Gate, nearly home." But the deadly pulsating drone was right above them. "Quick here's an open door, let's go down into the cellar." People (most people) left their front doors open so anyone caught in a raid could take shelter with them in the very deep cellars that most houses had, especially in Forrest Gate. About eight people were sitting there and all welcomed the newcomers. Hot cocoa and sandwiches were given. The bombs kept falling. 'Ack-ack' – guns on the backs of lorries were tearing through the streets. The huge guns in the park opposite the house were roaring when Janie suddenly stood up. "We must get out of here at once," she cried. "Please listen, we are all in danger."

The woman of the house asked Alan to calm Janie down. "this night has been too much for her, you'll be killed by the flack (the flack from the guns was red hot iron) from the guns, if not the bombs if you go out." She said, but on her insistence out they went, Alan was not pleased to face the onslaught. The brewery, on the corner was on fire, bottles shattering in the heat. Bottles of beer were flying through the air like missiles, could be deadly, and whisky, rum, wine, flowing like a golden stream in the gutters. The search lights had all held the silver plane in their grasp despite its twisting and turning in all directions. They reached Janie's home and ran through to the dugout.

"Thank God you're safe," Victoria said.

"Dad's not been home since he left this morning," Milly remarked. "And the docks are getting it bad."

It was all over by the time Bill returned. Blackened, hungry, tired, he went to bed. Victoria said to Janie, "Take this cake round to those kind people who sheltered Alan and yourself yesterday and thank them." (A whole weeks rations of butter, which was only one or two ounces per person, was used to make the cake.)

"Yes Mum." And she went. But the house had been hit, it had gone and the occupants lay dead under sheets of tarpaulin in the street. The rocking chair remained empty. Where Alan had gone, no one knew. Alan never knew what a lucky escape he had as she never saw him again. She had news of him that he had arrived home safely.

Milly had a baby girl, first grandchild for Victoria and Bill. Patsy was her name a child born during the war. Life still went on regardless of the all engulfing chaos of war. "We must be getting old wife," said Jack.
"Speak for yourself," she answered with a smile. "Plenty of years left in us yet I hope. The boys will be thrilled to hear they are now uncles."

"Well it will be great to see them tomorrow, a whole weekend with them. What a lovely old couple to have invited us to their cottage. As for that Farmer working the boys like that, I'd love to tell him a thing or two," said Bill.

"It's hard for us all in times like this. Labour on the land must be hard to find," said Victoria. Presents from Milly and Janie, for Ted and George were packed with lots of love and kisses.

Things all in all were not so bad for the Reynolds family. At least they still managed to get a roof over their heads. Night after night the heavy raids continued, but also the devastation. Entering Algate East Station, one of many across London to have the homeless start to bed down, from as early as two o'clock in the afternoon, joined after working hours by those looking for safe shelter (there were centres with food to feed them, yet the toilet and showers were few after all these centres were used for light sports before the war, not hundreds of homeless people). So the people heading for home, thanked their lucky stars they still had one to go to. Then it happened. A thousand pound delayed action bomb - which came slowly down by parachute this enabled people to see where they would land -at the back of the Reynolds dugout. It was a huge bump. The first they knew of it was when Uncle Max came shouting, "Get out! get out! run for it! don't stop for anything, you've only got a few minutes!" So off they went to one of the centres and would they now be joining the homeless? But the bomb was diffused ten days later by some very brave men.

Can one ever write about such times and picture them in one's mind, without a few tears falling for the heartbreak and misery of war that faced people day and night, on land, sea and in the air. Can one see it? One can certainly feel it. It's in everyone of us, the spirit to live, fight if need be and survive. Yet there is always the funny side, the 'cons' as they were called. There's one in every family it is said. Well one was right there in the Reynolds family. Not a family member, but brought in by one, thinking he was doing them a good turn.

Wars bring shortage and here stood the man who could be the answer to most women's prayers. From inside his coat he brought forth packets of silk stockings. The girls were joyous at this sight after months of having to coat their legs in a tanning lotion and an eyebrow pencil to draw a seam up the back of the legs. Whenever they put on a dress to go to a dance or out with the 'man of the moment', which was rare these days, there was always the stains from the lotion to worry about. Oh the lovely feeling of silk against one's legs again. He drew a pair from one packet. You'll not find better than these 'sheer silk' like cobwebs. The price was higher and he'd need a few coupons, those so precious clothing coupons. They bought for themselves and for some family members. Did he know of anyone who had batteries for these torches. No, he'd make enquires. Must go! good luck!. So a dance for the girls at Billy Lane's air force base, out came the precious stockings. Yes! There's one fool every minute it is said, and the shock on Janie's face said it all. "Look Mum! Look at this!" She held a pair of the precious stockings high in the air. One leg was too small to put on a child, the other she could manage both her legs in it. "And what's more they were all like it." The laughter was so infectious it was impossible not to join in. Oh well, back to the lotion and eyebrow pencil.

Poor Janie, she was always getting her words mixed up. Victoria asked her if she would go to the corner shop, as she was making cakes and wanted 'Eiffel Tower bun flour'. The shop, as usual, was full of people. "Yes Janie, what can I do for you today?" asked the Shopkeeper.

"Mum wants a packet of effin bun flour." Replied Janie. A roar of laughter came from those inside the shop.

"Oh, she does, does she? Well tell her I don't stock it."
"They don't stock it Mum."
"Of course they do! What did you ask for?"

"effin bun flour." Victoria clapped a hand over her

mouth to stop her laughter, for swear words were a no-no.
"It's 'Eiffel Tower' Janie!"

Looking back Janie could see why Vincent was always secretly laughing at her. But Bill, would often come out with a few remarks himself. Paper shortage had been around and it seemed toilet rolls would be scarce. "That's awful. What are we going to do?" asked Milly.

"That's easy, use newspaper," said Bill, "And people can all walk around with yesterday's news printed on their arse." So these terrible days brought laughter and what would we do without it.

Chapter LII

For some time, vivid dreams had awoken Janie from her sleep. She seemed to be in the past and at times, in the future. Reports had been coming in from pilots of seeing UFO's, but there had also been reports from ordinary civilians who had seen them as well. This was hush-hush, for anyone who even mentioned that they believed such things were considered, bluntly, 'off their rocker'. Ever since the encounter in the country when she was eight, Janie's psychic abilities were growing stronger and stronger and she was by now having a lot of dreams of the future. So when some of her dreams came true - either in newspaper reports or in the lives of people around, she never spoke a word about them. Neither had she mentioned the fast objects she had seen since a child crossing the sky. How little we know about the Universe and its inhabitants, she thought. Unfortunately UFO's were not the only things that hovered in the skies, there were plenty of man-made ones coming down with devastating effects, which now made Janie's Grandma Annie , her Auntie Mary and family, along with hundreds of others, homeless.

Chapter LIII

'Our boys' were seen in large numbers around old London town. The New Zealanders, Australians and Canadians we called 'our boys' because once more they had come home to help out. They were the breath of fresh air to tired old London and its worn out look.

After a while, a notice in the papers asking people to send in their names and address to be put on a notice board at the camp site's and how many they could manage, for the boys going on leave. Victoria wrote that three would be great. The Canadians each wrote back telling a bit about themselves. They were in the air force in the parachute branch and would love to spend their leave with the Reynolds family if accepted. So Jake, Claude (a French Canadian) and Murry Spriggs arrived in due course.

The house in Forrest Gate had large rooms upstairs and down. Unfortunately though, over the back wall was a large cemetery. Bill had had a terrible job at first, trying to rid the kitchen of ants – hundreds of them, loving everything they could find. Finally he won the battle, much to the relief of the family. Bill went to meet the lads, as he called them, at the main station. They were grateful to be with a family again and have some home cooked meals.

Although most housewives found the rations were pitifully inadequate, still they managed to feed their family. The boys had been given coupons to pass on to the lady of the house, which mostly covered all their needs. Jake, a tall handsome blonde haired man, was married and proud to show photos of his family. Claude had a trace of the French accent. He could speak the language fluently. He was short and jolly. Murry was tall, very good looking and knew it. But all three were what any mother would love to call a son. Victoria received food parcels from their parents back home. She was grateful to them and they in return were pleased to hear about their sons in the UK. Most of the family members came to visit them and a small party was held for one of their birthdays. A great sing song around the piano! Victoria playing and Bill on the drums. Both the piano and drum had survived so far in the blitz. This was to be their last leave though but no one knew it at the time.

Chapter LIV

Bill had come home after long hours and heavy bombing at the shipyards. He had just gone to bed, when a terrible wailing reached all their ears. Up the stairs went everyone, for a clear view of the cemetery could be seen. Whatever could have happened to cause such wailing. "Charlie! oh my Charlie! help me to decide what to do." More wailing could be heard. Bill got up.

"I've bloody well had enough of this." he said. He too came to look over the fence and there by a tombstone green with age and covered in moss, knelt a young woman. Whatever would a young person have to do with a grave as old as the hill, Bill questioned. Up went the wailing.

"Oh Charlie! oh Charlie what shall I do?" Bill angrily

shouted:

"I'll give you bloody Charlie if you don't shut up. I'm trying to get some sleep"

Still kneeling she looked up then reached for her handbag and still kneeling, brought her powder puff out and patted her face. Not a tear had fallen from her eyes. Standing up, she walked away. With a long sigh of relief, Bill went back to bed. It caused much laughter. All went to the station with the lads and waved them goodbye. By now they were part of the family.

"Come again soon," they called. There was some news about the Dutch and Canadians, parachuting over Holland which was in German hands? But not a word was heard of them, even though Victoria had written to enquire. Many years later, when one of her grandchildren was going to Toronto, Victoria gave her Murry Spriggs address. She wrote back. It had been a grand old house but now almost derelict. What became of them? Victoria guess the worse?

So war brought people from the four corners of the world in contact, who may never have met each other and they leave behind something of themselves – laughter, love, sadness.

It was cold, oh so cold. The window panes were covered in ice. Fuel was short, coal was short. It was useless pleading to the coal man tipping a sack of coal through the grate into the deep cellar below. His blackened face showed his despair. For the question must have been at every delivery. "Sorry missus. It's the miners you see – gone fighting the war." And who could blame them. If one is to be killed, better above ground than below I say."

"What a misery! We had to wait three weeks for one measly sack of coal and how long will it last? This weather chills one to the bone," said Victoria.

Shipping was also disappearing with our brave men to the bottom of the deep seas. They were hunted down by packs of u-boats.

"Starve them out!" was Hitler's orders.

One froze going to bed. Getting up and going to work, old bits of wood lying on bombed sites, the scattered bits of coal on the road, even any old chairs that could be spared, all disappeared into the fire. People took to going to bed in their oldest clothes, warm bricks by the one fire in the kitchen, wrapping them in towels to warm their feet in bed. One would kick the brick during the course of the night and a yell and a limp next morning. Yes, bricks could be weapons, in such a confined space.

Rubber bottle's had long gone, with most essential items – batteries for torches took their turn near the fire just to get that bit more use from them. Another torch had to be purchased (they had very limited life). To walk the black out in a pea-soup fog was just life threatening as anything falling from the sky. Step into a curb, a car or bus might hit you. Walking on the pavement one could hit an iron lamp post (no light of course) and there was many of them. Then there was crossing a busy road, traffic lights were dimmed, drivers had to be alert. Buses crawled along, very brave men holding a flamed piece of wood, walked a short space in front of it. What a strain to place on the bus driver. Everything was in short supply.

News on all fronts was bad. People came to dwell more - underground station platforms became camping grounds after rush hour in the morning. By night, women, children and babies were eating, fighting and sleeping. Men and women soaking wet from the terrible weather joined their families. Canteens became part of the scene for hot tea and soup. Radios blared the latest news and music. Homeward bound workers took all this into their daily routine and reaching home just as the air raid warning started, took their food to the dugout for another heavy night, hoping for a few quiet nights' sleep in a bed again.

Milly complained, "Still no news from Arthur."

"And can you wonder at it. Look what he must be going through," said Victoria.

News from North Africa was grim as was everything else on the battle fronts - in the sky, on the sea, on the land.
"The powers that be; buried their heads in the sand and hoped Hitler and his mob would disappear," said Bill "And look where it's got us. Don't worry girl, you'll get news soon."

And that very day the postman's rat-tat-tat sounded and four or five letters were pushed though the letter box. One for Janie from Vincent telling her as much about India as the censorship would pass.

"It's great hearing from him to know all's well," she said.

For she felt they had become in a way, soul mates. Janie shut the door behind her hanging on to the railings outside the houses, grateful for the sand the council workers had thrown on the roads and pavements much earlier. She slip-sloped her way to work with other passengers, who sat reading their morning papers or hanging on to the train straps, as the train stopped at a station a flurry of people got off and on. It was business as usual for one must work to live.

It was Saturday morning and Milly met Janie to buy a few things. They had just reached Woolworths in Aldgate East when the whining of a plane made them look up. It was coming straight at them. The hate in the pilot's eyes could be seen through his flying goggles. Janie's eyes locked on to his, held her to the spot. Milly pulled her to the ground as he machine gunned them, the bullets hitting the wall above their heads. He then headed to the round-a-bout on the busy street corner killing a policeman who was directing the traffic before heading back high into the clear blue sky. Only then did the air raid warning sound. The bullets may still be embedded in that Woolworths wall. What also remained with Janie was the terrible hatred she had seen in that pilot's eyes. So that's what they were up against. But why? They were the aggressors.

The BBC announced, "A lone raider" had killed a policeman. What a beginning to a new year. Not to be out done, Hitler sent us a New Years present. The warning had just started when hundreds of incendiaries descended on London, landing on roof tops, in back gardens, spouting, twisting small fire bombs of destruction. Everyone rushed to put out the ones on the ground and cover them before they exploded, dirt, sand, don't get too near. But fire had started in the roof. The incendiaries burnt down what bombs had failed to do this past year. The Reynolds family home, just one fire, joining many, as London started to burn. By morning, a smouldering heap was all that remained. The family had escaped over the back fence, from the fierce heat.

So once more down but not out, Bill looked for a roof over his family's head. Uncle Max, took them to a centre, but Milly and little Patsy stayed with Aunt Grace.

The house in Willow Grove was a house ugly and unloved, for in the food cupboard was an orange box. The open fire place in the kitchen was broken. Wall paper yellow and water stained smelling, hung from the walls. Did this worry Bill? Not one bit. "It's a roof over our heads wife." And in what little time he had from work and raids, he began to transform it. And for the first time since the war had been declared, Victoria who had never claimed war damage (because other people needed it more) was in line waiting her turn for help.

Yes there was talk that many raids would be a build up to invasion and that an attempt will be made soon. Well they failed the first time! It had been put around that the Germans had met a wall of fire oil poured into the sea. Many believed it despite the denial of those on high. Was such a menacing new year ahead? And what could they do about it? Hitler, it was said, would keep all Arian women, girls of child bearing age, young men would be put to work. The rest would be disposed of and he had no qualms (for now it had been a way of life for him for sometime). Enough to make one fight to the end, don't you think? It was a critical year ahead for all.

Some wonderful news putting some of Hitler's speed and perfect organisation, our boys were outside Tobruk. It was certain about the Italian defeat. The German official commented that 'while the British gain a military victory, the Italians, is a moral victory'. Well worn propaganda like 'Italians make love not war'. War it seems lasts longer. Theirs was well and truly on the way out and what's more they welcomed it.

The marching Romans of the past had brought many ideas and built many roads on their way across the world. They did not belong to the Hitler of today.

Still the invasion could happen. It was put around 'only three days to go' if the good weather sets in. Then came the announcement over the BBC, the governments warning to housewives to stock their invasion larders. What with? Italian sardines? (Just before war was declared there was ship load of Italian sardines available on every shelf in the country – no one like them for they were awful to eat.) For it was only those who had plenty of money could visit the East End and buy what East Enders could not afford until pay day. The Rich Invasion, had been going on and off – leaving empty shelves until the next deliveries which could be weeks away, depending on our ships making the hazardous crossing - not only on the high seas, but sometimes through the English Channel. For the loss of men and ships brought despair to many. The lull in the blitz was wonderful. The full moonlit nights would bring comment.

"They're sure to be over tonight. You mark my words." Janie confided in Rose, the dog. But Rose couldn't care less for she was loving her walks as Janie loved the spring flowers, blooming even on bombed sites. Her birthday was soon! Ted and George had been up for a week only on the understanding that they must return. My how they had grown! This war had been tough on the children. The tears had been shed when it was time to leave. "Come boys," Bill's voice sounded a little hoarse, "We can't miss the train, and it's a long journey and besides another lull like this you'll be home again." Still they miss them so much.

Bill was on his way home and seeing a queue outside

the corner shop asked what it was for "Birdseed mate" the man replied Hurrying back home Bill returned with a brown paper bag. A well-to-do man dressed in a suit approached Bill and asked Bill about the queue, Bill reiterated Birdseed mate! The man returned to the waiting car and the passenger in the car looked askance at him. "Birdseed Sir?" he said. This man himself was none other than Winston Churchill. It's reported that after he looked around at the devastation surrounding these people after a hard day's work, they were willing to queue no matter how long, for birdseed. This, it is said, brought tears to the eyes of Winston Churchill.

Bill was pleased with his share, for his three canaries and two budgerigars were near starvation. "What's a posh car doing here," stated Bill, as he gratefully fed some seeds to his birds, for everyone knew the Battle of the Atlantic being momentously fought, meant survival. No one, just no one, even thought of that. But of the brave men involved, Uncle Charlie was one, and Grandma and Granddad feared for him. Sid also in the Royal Marines, had been sent to Egypt. He sent letters but little was in them regarding his duties. "So long as he was well,"

   That night, Germany's spring offensive began. It was the heaviest raid of the year so far and worst was to follow. Janie had little to celebrate on her eighteenth birthday. Many girls of her age were now allowed to join the armed forces – not women. So when the quiet times came she took driving lessons to give her a head start, so to speak. Very few people had ever owned a car and the way things were, had no desire to do so. Besides the bombing, petrol was hard to get. Even a new baby grand piano was offered for fifty pounds, by a couple hell bent on getting out of London. Very few people were interested in such things, for tomorrow was another day which no one could count on. At the moment, the call up of women of twenty and twenty one, and men of forty and forty one, was announced for next month. Married women with children were exempt.

The loss of the war ships, Prince of Wales and the Repulse, who's arrival at Singapore was still so recent that the loss seemed at first almost incredible. People were stunned into silence, sheer disbelief. Having to first absorb the initial shock from Sunday evening radio announcement of the Japanese attack on Pearl Harbour, and then, anger, at the big battleship's disappearance and the Repulse – people wanted to know why this had been allowed to happen.

The sudden entrance of Japan into the war, the United States declaration of war on Germany and Italy, plus Hitler's biggest mistake, Russia came as a shock to all. The anger over the loss of those two ships would not die down. Admiral Phillips' judgement in deciding that aerial escort was not needed because the weather was overcast; brought a response from the newspaper cynics to hope the High Command isn't banking on the chance that the Germans will pick a rainy day for an invasion of this island.

Christmas was but a few weeks away, and so far the streets were empty – toys are scarce and expensive and wrapping paper, was at an all time low. But Christmas this year was of no consequence it just came and went. Bill and Victoria spent two days with Goerge and Ted in the Country. Milly with little Patsy spent a quiet Christmas at home with Janie.

Janie was on her way to visit Aunt Mary. What with the fall of Singapore and thousands of our men prisoners of war, George her son was them; Aunt Mary needed some companionship. Janie remembered going to the station with his wife and daughter (at their request) for he was on overseas departure. So waving goodbye was the last time for them. He was on the infamous Japanese railway and died like many of the poor souls at the mercy of a soulless enemy. Aunt Mary refused to believe it. His army pal, who had after the war, survived the ordeal, came to reassure her that he was by his side at the end - this helped her to accept his passing.

Still girls and machines worked through the day, leaving their benches only at the last minute of a raid warning. Janie with others went to the roof top, 'plane spotters' and pressed an alarm for all to rush down to the shelters. At the fall of Poland (whose brave people fought against two aggressors, Germany and Russia) there was an influx of Polish refugees. So many Polish men took up their trade in tailoring. At first sound of an air raid warning they would turn almost panic stricken look for the shelter pushing everything and everyone out of their way. Many could not speak English, so the one that could, was shown a shelter deep into the basement, for them. For a long time since war began, army, navy and air force uniforms had joined the railway and busmen uniforms on the conveyor belts which had been set to maximum speed, so much that the girls complained all the time, for they were tired. If there had been a lull in the raids the girls were expected to work overtime. They always needed the extra money, but these days of shortage, left little incentive to work, beside the British was almost sinking with uniformed men and refugees, free French, Polish, Canadians, New Zealanders.

Since the Japanese war, the Australians had gone to their side of the world and fighting on many fronts with other Commonwealth men. Australia would be attacked. Now the Americans had landed more pay, silk stockings, coffee, tea, chocolate and" yes mam, no mam" and the music and jive.

Poor old war torn England was jolted back to Jeeps on the roads, all hotels and restaurants fully booked for plenty of money had arrived with them. Also, "I will show you how to win a war gusto." "Yes, but where were you when we needed you most? When we stood alone?" All the same, we still needed and were thankful they were on our soil.

With all that manpower around, why in heavens name did the girls at work, start putting the other girls names and address into the trouser pockets of the uniforms? The daily mail, delivered many letters from these service men to the girls who had revived a boost to their morale these days and were taking time off from work to go to the West End. American clubs and the cinema had opened with longer hours.

Janie had also received a few letters, some had enclosed a photo of themselves, which she passed round for comment at home. One was from a Donald Brooks, who he stated would love to receive a letter from her. He was a teacher in a secondary school before joining up. As usual, Jack made a few comments on the photos - "Oh that one has a boozer's nose. I'd watch him girl!" Or, "Not that one, he has a long nose! He must be married!" And all the time wishing he could be back in uniform. The First World War should have been enough for him, and his job was too important, so he couldn't go anyway, like many war workers on day and night shift. Where would England be without them?

Milly was now working on the mechanics of American Jeeps. She enjoyed doing it. The dependence allowance she received from the army was too small for herself and her growing child. For years, when people married (war time) and husbands were away, mostly their wives and children (if any) stayed with family, for comfort and support. Even after the war, it would be years sometimes, before a house was available. So Victoria took to looking after Patsy who was as happy with her life (but it would be good if daddy came home Mummy!). But at that moment in time, Daddy was busy fitting a string to his ukulele thrilled that at last he had found a wire to fit. At that moment the eighth army communication had grounded to a halt. Arthur, blissfully went on singing, playing and fighting his way with the boys towards Italy, unaware till later the power of 'Ukulele' (The Hawaiian name is jumping flea – 'some flea' as Winston Churchill would have muttered.

So Donald Brooks wrote to Janie and on his leave came to see her. They got on very well, the family liked him. So of course they started going out. It being war time and all that, people met people. This continued for a while, suddenly no news from him – must have gone overseas, she thought, even so, still no letters.

The war moved on and so did Janie. She had joined the N.A.A.F. (Navy, Army and Air Force) as a driver. Jack, thrilled, he had a daughter in uniform, went with her to the main station. Putting her case down he said, "Be good. Don't let the side down," and stood on the platform till the train puffed its self out of sight.

On reaching her destination and making inquiries as to the camp, she was told of a short cut through the woods. The damp smell of the woodland greeted her. She entered it bringing memories of her childhood flooding back with the Davenport family and John their son, who had met his death early in the war. So much had happened since then. Here she was with butterflies in her stomach, or was it hunger? (And so many mattresses lying amongst the leaves, surely the homeless of London hadn't come this far out). She felt at peace, yet an eerie feeling permeated the woods. Shivering, she hurried on and was relieved to reach a lane. A lorry had just turned the corner and now stopped beside her. Hello NAAFI, "I'm on my way to the camp hop in." Gratefully, she accepted. By his uniform he was in the air force. "I'm Ronald. This is your first camp?" She nodded.

"I'm Janie."

"Well Janie, what camp?" She looked puzzled. "There are two – army on the left and air force on the right."

"Oh, army please." He drew to a sudden halt.
"Then this is it." She got off. He handed her suitcase down to her. "See you Janie," he said and took off before she could answer.

He had taken her to the back entrance of the kitchen. This puzzled her, anyway she entered and the scene seemed one of chaos. A huge table crammed to the very edges – what a mess! She thought Mum wouldn't dream of cooking with such a clutter. After a perfunctory glance, they all got on with their jobs. The cook red faced, hot anger barely contained was rushed off her feet. Each time the girls carried the numerous plates through the heavy doors, they caught glimpses of the row of soldiers waiting for their meal. Janie sat on the nearest chair, what was she doing here? She had signed up as a driver, oh well, she'll wait it out. And wait it out she did. When the rush had died down and most of them had flopped down into the nearest chairs, they suddenly remembered her. The cook stood over her. "Show me your papers."

"I'm supposed to give them to the managers," said Janie.

"Well you can't, so you'll have to give them to me."
"Then I'll wait until she gets back."

"Oh what have we got here girls!?" Much laughter followed. Janie felt at that moment she had made a very big mistake. And the air force would have been better. The cook opened the letter. "I asked for a kitchen hand," she said "And look at what they have sent me." They took a look and roared with laughter at the immaculate person in front of them. Even her proud countenance was enough.

"I'd signed on as a driver," said Janie.

"In this mob, you do and go where they send you," replied the cook. "Read the small print if you don't believe me. I'll have to think where to put you, better stay where you are." One girl gave Janie a cup of tea and some sandwiches. Most of the girls disappeared.

"They've got a few hours off until this evening, then it's work until late, again. My name's Helen."
"Mine's Janie." Once again it seemed everyone had forgotten about her. The cook had that's for sure, and still no managers.

"Time for bed!" Helen said to her. "Sorry about today. Has anyone told you where to sleep?" Wearily Janie shook her head. "Better come with me, to our lodgings, the landlady won't like it. Four of them headed towards their billets, with Janie dragging behind with her heavy suitcase.

Unfortunately things went from bad to worse if that was possible. The landlady was most upset on seeing Janie. "This has got to stop. It'll mean five of you to a bed (the beds were large and there was normally two girls up the top and two at the bottom – top and tailing) the health inspector will have something to say about this. And I can't keep changing the sheets as they're almost threadbare as it is."

"The old bat" Helen said when she had gone. "Look Janie, there's a dance on, put on a dress and come with us. It'll do you good and you really can't stay here by yourself." So Janie complied, the only bright spot of the day, she thought. How wrong she was. As soon as she entered she was asked to dance. A new face she thought – but he would keep asking her to dance. He certainly wasn't her cup of tea thought Janie. Helen came and whispered into her ear. "Now you've done it good and proper. That's the cook's boyfriend, just look at her face."

"The end of a perfect day," groaned Janie. No not quite – five to a bed was no picnic. Janie tried to sleep hanging on to the edge of the bed with her legs hanging out.

So this went on, the cook gave her all the nasty jobs to do, scrubbing the large pantry, which looked like it hadn't seen water in a long time. She was put collecting the dishes in the large canteen, in a huge basket she filled it up – bending over to lift the basket, someone pinched her bottom and she dropped the lot, the cups, saucers, plates, crashed to the floor. Her face red with embarrassment, she bent to pick the broken pieces up – some of the soldiers helped her. The cook greeted her with jeers

"Can't do anything can you?"

"A transfer would be wonderful," answered Janie.

"Bless my soul, she really did exist." The Manageress arrived at last. Downcast, the cook followed her into the office where they sat talking. Tea was taken in. The cook came out shaking her head.

"I just can't get through to her, she thinks she's jinxed. It appears two more American planes didn't make it back last night, friends of hers, that makes six planes of her group this week. She said she is jinxed and bad luck will follow her and those around." Janie thought 'welcome to my world' for her transfer had not come through. When all had died down, Janie asked to see her. She found a plump fifty five year old woman who was possibly having the time of her life, living it up two or three nights of the week at the American Club. None of this was ever reported. Helen told Janie, they all felt sorry for her and covered it up. What could she do for Janie? She would talk to cook. So Janie had no bed to sleep in. The landlady said she couldn't return tonight. Well she would let Janie know later on in the day.

"You've got a bed," said the cook, "We have given Madge two weeks leave."

The kitchen hand had a tiny room to herself due to the fact she had to get up at five thirty to light the kitchen range, take cook a cup of tea and toast at six thirty and lay the girls breakfast table. Then wash everything up – cups, plates, pans, saucepans, one could go on, heavy iron hardware, the first till after lunchtime, then on again at five o'clock till gone nine o'clock. Well that went well from bad to worse. The pain from having her hands and arms in water, from day till night, except a few hours break in between was terrible. The rash she developed was from the soda in the water. She was very grateful for the narrow bed she had in her tiny closet, called a bedroom. So this was war. Madge came back off "leave" Janie was put on the food counter. Janie was to wait until they sent a proper kitchen hand, which was a whole month later. She sighed with relief, when she finally arrived.

Now they sent her to the other camp. Standing at the crossroads waiting for the lorry to pick her up, she mused on the facets of life. How one's fate, could be made on a simple decision. Taking the left road, instead of the right, could change one's life, like war had changed hers and thousands more. She could walk away right now, but knew she wouldn't. It was not in her nature to walk away, even if what she was doing wasn't that great. Someone had to do the work and the thought of those conveyor belts at the factory, was never and never would be of her choice.

So she waited for the air force lorry – might be Ronald at the wheel! She soon found out (no, not this time) had he also moved on and on. She was due for a leave, home sweet home, no bombs had fallen near the camp, though planes passing overhead was more our own.

"Rose! Rose!" called Janie, but Rose did not come. "Mum, where's Rose?" Victoria faced her. "She followed you Janie on your last leave and we haven't seen her since. We made every effort to find her, for we also miss her. She is old and the roads are busy."
"But after all these years Mum!"

Chapter LV

At this camp kitchen, law and order was in place. A handsome young man received a friendly greeting from the girls. "What was an American soldier doing here?" He looked over at her.

"Well, well, what have we here," he drawled. She looked at him (He looked like he had just stepped off a movie screen). One of the girls drew her over to the window.

"Don't let him near you. The girl whose place you have taken is pregnant by him and he couldn't care less." Here she was to serve at the counter now full of airmen, and she had her own bed. Things were looking up.

It was hard work as usual and no matter how tired one was, if a dance was on the cards it made one's week. Her leave came round. She caught the train which was full of uniformed men as usual. The American soldier sitting opposite said, "Excuse me, mam, how many stations to Charing Cross?"

"Eight stations," she answered.

"Geeeee!!" he drawled, "You're sure technical." Janie, terribly shy, shone a brilliant red at receiving such attention. Silence reigned for a few more stations and then he again spoke. "How about coming to the American Club with me and having some lunch?" He looked a very nice person. He had a lovely smile and no doubt he was lonely and far from home. Again she thought one decision was all it took, which could change her life, but she declined. Janie was very self-conscious of her appearance in her uniform; hers was a rough clothe against his refined Kakai and she would feel out of place at the American Club. . Later telling her mum about the invitation and the reason why she refused to go

"You should have accepted if he looked a nice person."

Sitting reading a book late in the evening, Janie wished she had and to this day often wonders what could have become of the encounter for their was definite chemistry between them.

Romantic encounter were common on the train; Janie was serenaded once by an officer from the Air Force on her way home one evening. The train was lite up with very low blue lights; Janie boarded the train and sat opposite this officer, she noticed him staring at her a lot. He started to whistle an old war time song 'Sweet and Lovely' Janie knew it was directed at her; face shone bright red in contrast to the blue lights. This was a source of amusement to the fellow passengers and a lot of laughter was to be heard across the carriage. After the Air Force Officer finished his romantic serenade everyone clapped and Janie did not know where to hide her face.

Whistling was very common at all times of the day and night; one could often here a lone whistler walking passed in the twilight hours. Some of the most beautiful whistling one could ever hear would fill the night with many musings.

Chapter LVI

It had been building up for some time; tanks, men together with all sorts of artillery. Over a year ago there was talk of a second front, Russia had been making loud noises for it to start. A lot of our ships had been sunk on their way to Russia. Poor Uncle Charlie was in freezing water once again. Saved by Iceland fishermen and taken to America, it would be a year or more before he was home again. Some of the coastal areas had been restricted to the public and permits obtained.

Janie was called to the manageress' office and told she was to report to head quarters at once. This she did, wondering what it was all about. She was told, "What you see, you don't repeat." Given her fare and permit and sent on her way.

The First World War camp had not been used for many years. She sensed the ghosts of the past all around her. The cast iron trays with handles, men ate their food off. There were the heavy cooking pots, the rough sleeping quarters, she was shown too. Many bunks, two very old wardrobes and as a bonus to help her on her way, was cockroaches. On opening one of the wardrobes, she felt for some hangers for her clothes. Cockroaches fell on her head and shoulders. Large brown shining, creepy-crawly insects that seem to resent the intrusion. Brushing furiously at her hair and shoulders she locked the wardrobe hoping to contain them and putting her clothes back into the suitcase, sat on the bed and looked at her surroundings. She was to have this room to herself, but felt that ghosts were sharing it with her. Hurrying out, she entered the kitchen. The large iron-range had many boiling pots on it, steam was everywhere. She went closer to peer a little into the pots and was horrified to see a mass of cockroaches trying to cling to the roof above the stove, but losing, so falling into the food below. Protein, no doubt! But she was not that desperate.

A woman entered and greeted her, "You're our new driver, I suppose. I'm the cook." Two army men carried produce in, "These are Jim and Bill and I'm Kate."
"Pleased to meet you, I'm Janie."
"Candy the other driver won't be long, she will show you what to do."

Candy made her appearance. By her very walk one could tell she was sure of herself and when she spoke it was the voice of private education. Janie was also well spoken having had singing lessons. She had won a scholarship to a school of music. Jack's words came back to her

"Sorry Janie, but we can't fish one and fail the other."

He meant well, bless him, she thought. Candy was relieved to see her.

"Help me fill the two urns up, bring the trays of cakes and sandwiches into the van. I'll get the cigarettes and sweets. We must leave soon."

An army officer gave a list to her and they were off. "We have to meet a convoy; they have been travelling from Scotland and need refreshments."

She then proceeded to tell Janie what prices to charge for the goods. They were lower than shop items. This was the first convoy of four that day so they would have to return to base depending on what was sold. They would have to travel a great deal.

Janie loved the open roads and countryside. Two hours later they met the convoy. It was all worthwhile. The men were grateful.

"Hi NAFFI!! you're always here when we need you. Got any Cigarettes? Got some stamps? I want to put a letter in your box, post it for me, there's a good girl!"

They knew what was ahead of them, though they joked and laughed. She could see the strain of the long journey was telling on them.

The pattern day by day increased and sometimes they would have to go back to base many times. The army camps were now all around. Camouflage, was the major word, for guns, huge guns and tanks were rolling in and hidden amongst the trees. Sometimes they were ordered to the firing ranges to get to know the troops and offer them some comfort in order to keep their morale up. There were only three women, Candy, the Cook and Janie amongst all these men. No entertainment here, just training and hard work for the big day was yet to come.

They had arrived at one of the firing ranges and had just finished serving the men and were waiting for the last of the cups to be returned. The men had returned to the range, when the Crown Sergeant came over.

"Which one of you ladies would have the guts to fire that machine gun." Candy said no thank you. "Come on," he said, "We'll never win the war with the likes of you, that's for sure." Candy was twenty nine years of age, "This might be in Janie's corner. Well you're younger than me Janie!" Reluctantly, Janie went with the Sergeant, all the men cheered her on.

Having instructed her on what to do, she was now lying low on the ground, her feet hard on the ground.

"That's right, press the trigger and aim at that board."

This she did but unfortunately no one had allowed for her slight form and the machine gun swung her around, now she was firing on the troops. They shouted and ducked low. An officer who had no doubt just arrived put his head up and shouted "Let go!!!" A bullet took his hat off. She let go, his face as white as a sheet. Was it anger or fear? He came, picked her up and shook her.

"You damn fool! You could have killed us all." Then he said in a shocked voice. "Janie, what are you doing here?"

It was Donald Brooks. A silence had spread over them all that was eerie, broken by Candy

"Come Janie, we must be getting back."

The anger still showed on Donald's face when she beat a hasty retreat.

Neither of them spoke on the way back, both were deep in their own thoughts. Oh dear, what had she done? She could have killed members of his Majesty's force. Would they have clapped her in jail? Of course they would. Poor Donald, what a way to have come back into her life! Well, she won't be seeing him again that's for sure. Who'd want a lethal girlfriend? She giggled at the thought. "It's not funny," snapped Candy, "We could be in a lot of trouble if he reports us. Where did you meet him anyway?"

"At one of life's crossroads," Janie answered.

During the war all the signs of the roads and stations were changed or taken away, because of spies or people taking pictures – it was difficult some times to know what station you were drawing into or what lane you were walking down- all sense of direction was lost.

Days passed, no one had spoken to them regarding the incident. They had gone to the shooting range as usual, different troops were there. So they were in the dark so to speak, as to the outcome to the sergeant. She hoped he would not lose his rank, but somehow knew he would.

By now, camouflage nets covered most things and still they met the convoys. It had been a very tiring day. Letting the heavy shutter down, Janie's hand was caught. She wasn't quick enough and it ripped her middle finger nail right off. She was lucky not to have lost her fingers. Blood was everywhere. Wrapping her hand in a tea towel, they headed for the medical centre. The guards at the gates let them in for headquarters was also there. The hill in front of them was very steep, troops were everywhere. Rude remarks on the walls and soiled sanitary pads hung by their loops on nails high on the walls – 'from now on, it would be a man's world'. The doctor was gentle and kind as he wrapped the finger up.

"Do you know Janie; you're my very first patient. I wish that you were my last."

Looking into his sad face, she gently put her hand on his in mutual sympathy for what lay ahead.

    She was unpacking the van at the end of the day, when Donald blocked her path. She was about to say sorry, when he demanded why she had not answered his letters? Not liking his tone of voice

"Just answer my question Janie!" "Why should I" she replied indignantly and walked passed him. So that was that.

    Candy had received a telegram, "...Missing, believed killed." Her now late husband after four years of marriage, but only one together now another casualty of war – just another number. Two weeks leave, drivers were in demand, so Janie would have to manage as best she could. This was impossible, so an army driver took Candy's place, leaving Janie free to deal with the troops. The driver wasn't sure where to go to meet 4B convoy (It was stated they had been hours on the road) taking the wrong lane they went into a paddock to turn around, but was hailed by an officer, with red stripes on his collar' also standing beside him was an American. The driver got out, stood to attention and saluted. The Officer said "Serve my men." By now the troops were coming towards the van. The driver turned to Janie and in blissful ignorance, she answered,

    "I have to meet 4B convoy."

    "You'll serve my men!" the officer demanded. Anger was now showing. He was used to being obeyed. "My orders are to meet convoy 4B! retorted Janie" The American solider at the officers side reminded her that one must obey orders at all time.
    Janie insisted " I HAVE GOT TO MEET 4 B CONVOY!!

The officer was too flabbergasted that this chit of a girl should answer him back and in front of his troops. The driver red in the face got in behind the wheel. The American came up at the side of the van, with a mischievous smile and a wink. They met the convoy, one of three. Janie filled up the van and retraced her steps. It was now four o'clock in the afternoon. At the sight of the van the men came running. But she must have been the last person the officer wanted to see.

"We'll soon be going," he said to his troops, "You can wait." They turned away. Janie knew they were longing for a cup of tea or coffee. They turned the van around to leave. The American was on her side of the van. He put his head into the open window and with a broad smile said, "Well you did your best." She told the family as much later.

"How was I to know it was General Montgomery and General Eisenhower!!

" There was a great deal of chatter around for the driver must have said something (another one of Janie's blunders) How Vincent would have laughed she thought.

Going home on leave was sad in a way. There was no Rose to come and greet her. She had followed after Janie on her last leave and was never seen again.

Chapter LVII

Poor Candy. She returned and got on with her job, which seemed never ending. Things were warming up, both at home and overseas. Letters were coming through from Arthur and Vincent was still sending letters to Janie. Granddad had a chest problem, which sometimes put him in hospital. Grandma had a lot of support from her family. So day by day, planes passed overhead and warnings sounded. Everyone got on with their jobs and tightened their belts. Food rations were being cut. Second hand clothes were now selling, also children's toys, chairs, tables – everything was still in very short supply. Newspapers had been curtailed a long time ago. Milk had been rationed for some time. Due to the farmers growing vegetables, grass for the cows had become scarce. Eggs had been seen once every three months, mostly for the sick, pregnant women and small children. Lease lend from America had been great – dried eggs (first every seen) made scrambled eggs a treat. All the time people knew something big was on the way.

Sometimes Donald and Janie came into contact within their work. Both were distant towards each other, until one day Donald stopped Janie and said

"Meet me when you have finished, say about eight o'clock by the first tanks." Not waiting for her reply, he turned and walked away. Would she go, no why should she? But then again, she had almost killed him and he never reported them. She would have to go if only to get it over with.

He was waiting for her. She knew he would ask why she had not answered his letters. So she got in first

"How could I answer letters that never came Donald? So now you know." She turned to walk away.

"Not so fast Janie. We had great times in the past; did they mean so little to you?"
"No, but this is wartime. You and I know that time is limited."
"Then let's make the most of the little time we have left."
"How can we? We cannot leave this camp."

"You will of course, I'm sad to say. Yes, I don't intend to leave without an answer from you one way of the other. You know how I feel about you." She did, but felt sick at what was ahead of him and hundreds more. Just look at Candy she thought. Janie found herself saying,

"Yes Donald." Both of them were silent.

"I will not hold you to it Janie, should I return." But somehow it was almost too much to bear and the tears ran down her face. He wiped them gently away. "We will no doubt be moving out any day now. But with luck we will come through." She nodded, not trusting herself to speak. They met when they could and were happy to have even that time together. Some days later, when she was on the range, he came. "It has come Janie. The next few days we are moving out." She had heard and had seen what was going on around her.

"We knew it would come." Most of the men she was serving also knew the time had come. For the feelings were tense and deeply felt.

"Must go," he said.

She and Candy were flat out serving the incoming

troops. The others were on their way out – cars, trucks, guns. The tanks had left during the night. One of the cars stopped in front of the van. Donald got out and she went to meet him. He took the badge out of his hat. "Remember me Janie!" and gave it to her. "Keep it my love, till I return. I'll send you a letter from France!" He hugged and kissed her.

"Good luck Donald. I love you!" shouted Janie. He got back into the car and waved as he joined the rest in line.

Her heart was filled with love for this heroic young man. He was so proud to go off and be of service to his country. His courage was common amongst the troops. Janie could not help thinking about the tragedy of wars. How people who were complete strangers could face each other on the battlefield and fight to the death. Had these people met under different circumstances they may have been friends, who knows?

Hitler had to be stopped that was for sure, but it was a shame it would cost the lives of so many innocent young men on both sides of the war.

The upper classes had gotten away with a lot, they took all their food and lived the high life while everyone else struggled and fought to keep hold of their liberty. Often the rich would look on from a distance; intellectual musing was a matter of entertainment for them. How different life would have been if everyone had access to the same level of education...

Chapter LVIII

Janie home on leave! Although the news of D Day came through on the radio a long time before, Victoria, Bill and Milly with little Patsy by her side and Janie stood in the garden as the whole neighbourhood were doing out of their doors, leaning from upstairs windows, cheering and waving as the great fleets of planes roared towards the coast.

"Give it to them boys," shouted Bill. The hundreds of planes carried gliders at their tails which were released before landing; not all the landings were happy ones. The sky became deafening and dim with waves of planes which one could mistake for large locusts.

A sudden silence descended over the watching people, for many husbands and sons could be passing overhead. And many no doubt thought of the boys who never returned from the beaches at Dunkirk.

Janie knew what lay ahead, the boys she had given tea and cigarettes to could be injured or lying dead right now. She remembered a convoy coming in late in the evening (mostly sold out, but enough tea to quench ones thirst). A captain stood with a group of his men in front of the van. One soldier asked her for a packet of cigarettes. She had sold out. "I have a few left in my pocket," she said (She was not a smoker but liked to offer them to others as was done at the time).

The captain said, "May I buy them from you." She shook her head and passed the packet to him. About five cigarettes remained. Taking them out he broke each cigarette into pieces that to Janie's mind would be difficult to hold, let alone smoke and gave as many as he could to his men, saving the smallest piece for himself. She passed a box of matches to the men and each lit the tiny piece in their mouth. One or two puffs was surely all they would get, she was impressed by the comradeship displayed by all. She watched as dusk fell on them, not wanting to disturb the scene that would forever remain in her memory.

But at this moment in time, Donald was with her, for she had a sinking feeling of his presence. She was being stupid, when things died down a bit they would be allowed to write, she thought. Silence still remained in houses, pubs, on the streets. The distant rumble of guns could be heard.

When Janie got back from her short leave, train loads of the wounded were already on their way to the hospitals. It was proof of the heavy toll on the men at the front and the people who had to treat the injured as one saw how bloody the returning men were through the train windows and at the stations on their way to the hospitals. The symbol of the Red Cross was on all trains and trucks. Women waiting at the crossings for these trains to pass didn't know whether to wave or cheer or cry. Sometimes they did all three.

Uncle Max called in for a cup of tea and a ten minute sit down. He talked more and had changed a great deal, no doubt due to his job as head warden. Speaking to Victoria, "I can see that a few of your neighbours have returned from the country." He was of course referring to the two houses opposite, whose windows had been boarded up all this time. The owners had the money to take themselves out of bomb range in the big blitz, but had moved back. They were now being regarded with a good deal of coldness by the shopkeepers and neighbours.

"But bombs are dropping again," said Victoria. She was

referring of course to the fire bombers last Tuesday. The German bombers were making sharp attacks leaving homes a heap of ashes, which kids and adults alike stood watching as if it were a Guy Fox night. The broken glass is being shovelled out of the gutters again. The crowds are taking shelter in the underground stations. And now Mr. Churchill's warning that pilotless planes and rocket shells might soon be heading towards England from the French coast. As if we hadn't enough to worry about right now.

But not so the youngsters who are having a great time collecting flutterers, the strips of silver foil which were dropped by the raiders to interfere with the detecting instruments that were part of London's defence. The silver strips hanging from trees, gutters on houses, lying in heaps on pavements, gave London a Christmas festive look, though tired out, bombed out, burnt out, short of everything, rationed nation was far from even wanting to think of what to put in the Christmas stockings.

As the brave men on all fronts fought the Germans and Japanese, the horrors of war were there for all to see. On the newsreels and in the painfully thin and ragged children being brought to our shores, told of starvation, misery and survival. The government warned over the air and in newspapers that the feeding and clothing of the people in the liberated countries would be a strain so severe that it would have to be shared by all, so that the cuts to our rations would begin in a few weeks. But at this time pilotless planes were being chased by our pilots over the southern coast and shot down but many reached London. One could hear the put-put of the engines. It was when the engines cut out the planes would then continue silently towards its victims.

Ted and George had pleaded so hard to come home that Victoria and Bill went down to see the old couple who had taken such care of them. Her husband was not all well and was now taking most of her time. So back they came, doodle bugs (beginning of today's rockets) as they were called still flying over head or landing close by.

Ted had grown tall and strong and George looked well and happy to be home. Janie still with the troops, for now most of our island was filling up with the Americans on their way to the Western front with the other Commonwealth troops. But she managed to get up for a day to hug and kiss them. Little Patsy was nearly five years of age, loved having them around.

People were returning to London from war work in the country for the doodle bugs being shot down over them were causing lost hours of work and great damage. So as it was to be expected, as a shortage of housing, rents were high and house prices were beyond the dreams of many. Mr. Churchill's promise of a thousand '(h)ouses' a day for returning troops and the homeless seemed as far away as ever. For the doodlebugs had now been joined with the rockets which at night were incandescent, plunking out of the blue with a truly appalling explosion which leaves the air in shock waves with the people.

As yet no word from Donald and Janie's sinking feeling which had come over her on D Day was she felt a warning. Everyone was now saying 'after the war' or when the lights go on again, talking of course about the European war. There was still the Japanese to deal with and what was going on over there island by island was terrible news, as was on the seas. How many men, women and children must suffer before the end was in sight?

George had taken a job – a few hours after school – as a delivery boy for the local butcher. The shilling worth of meat allowed per person made the humble sausage highly prized. From under the counter wrapped in newspaper and sent to a special customer. Now, hours later, George had not returned, sending someone round to Victoria's house to enquire for by now he was very worried.

When Victoria heard, she said, "Oh my God!" A few rockets have fallen in that direction. They hurried towards the place where reports were coming in of the injured and killed. It was a total mess. George was not to be seen or found. Uncle Max joined the search. It was toward dusk in the evening when he was found wandering through the streets in a terrible state. It seemed the huge blast had blown him some distance away. He was so lucky to be alive.

Allied troops were now reported only fifteen miles from Berlin and workmen had started pulling down the surface shelters in the streets, signs that VE Day is not far ahead. People can now walk out their doors without the dread of V-2s which fell repeatedly on London. And now the order came to turn up the lights.

Milly thought of Arthur coming home after all those years. But for Janie the news she had been dreading, Donald, like thousands of brave men had been a casualty of war. Inwardly Janie felt her grief as so many mothers, wives and sweethearts did. The loss through all families around the world was too terrible to contemplate. Nothing is simple in life and war has its own way of ending. For more was to come. The horrors of the concentration camps were revealed, the terrible treatment of prisoners of war by the Japanese. There were many prisoners here working in the fields – healthy, well fed and getting double the rations of the suffering nation. As the horrifying photographs came, the shock to the public had been enormous. No doubt the horrors of war hidden away would be revealed in the years to come.

When the family came down to breakfast, in the last hours of peace, in September 1939, a violent thunderstorm broke over the city. Victoria, so strong, had rushed into the cellar.

Now nature was taking a hand in a violent thunderstorm. Thunder rolled, violent flashes of lightening struck the earth, in the early hour of May 8th 1945. And of course, Victoria could be found sitting on her chair in the cellar. The war had now ended.

People danced and sang in Trafalgar Square and Piccadilly Circus and hugged each other. They stood in hundreds waiting for the King and Queen and two Princess's too make their appearance on the balcony of the Palace. Cheering, waving, when they did so. When Winston Churchill made his debut, roars were as loud as thunder. "Winnie, Winnie," they chanted (an endearing name). A slightly formal official broadcast had been made earlier in the day. Now he stood in front of them for all to see.

"My dear friends, this is your victory," he said.

To us all, Winston Churchill is and always will be our man of the century.

The bells rang out all over the country and towns. To sleep peacefully in ones bed was indeed well overdue. The streets at night were still dark for the lights had to be adjusted. For a while, people still pulled their heavy curtains as darkness fell. The habits of five and half years were hard to forget. Children were seeing lights in shop windows for the first time. What will they think when the lights of London go on again.

But we must now turn our thoughts to war, to fierce fighting on land, sea and in the air. The hot steaming jungles where men fought and slept, not seeing the enemy half the time for they were hidden under the growth and high in the tree tops. The battles in the air and on the sea were heavy and the gaining of islands was costing hundreds of lives.

Vincent was by now in Burma, so letters were scarce. Janie had met Brenda on a bus today, for now Brenda was issuing bus tickets. As usual, her smart remarks made the passengers laugh. Janie thought she looked good in her uniform for it was one of the smartest uniforms out of them all. She thought the fire brigade next. Brenda had married an airman of some financial means and the last she had news of her, she was living in a mansion in the country. But it was like putting a wild bird in a cage, for it was only waiting to escape. Which it seems she had.

"Hi Janie, what are you doing this way?"
"I might ask you the same question," said Janie.
"Oh, Sean's in Burma. He's been there sometime. So is Vincent, I hear maybe in the same camp?"
"Could be Brenda" replied Janie.
"Still with the troops Janie?" asked Brenda.
"Yes, we have a notice up asking for volunteers to go to Germany." replied Janie.
"And are you?" asked Brenda.
"Not at this moment Brenda." As Janie got off the bus, Brenda said,

"Sorry to hear about Donald." She waved, pressed the bell and the bus moved on.

That's what life is all about thought Janie as she stood watching the bus till it turned the corner. Moving on, should one go left, right or straight ahead at the crossroads of life.... She sighed, reflecting on the moment, it was all too much, for now she was on her way to visit Granddad, who was very ill in hospital. Most of the family had already made their visit. Turning into the hospital, she hoped he had improved. A nurse was by his side, when she had left. Janie drew up a chair.

"They are lovely," he whispered, nodding towards the carnations and pinks she was holding.
"Your favourite flowers Granddad." Remember you grew them on your allotment before the war."
"It seems a very long time ago Janie." She had to lean closer to hear him.

"You'll soon be well, you'll see." said Janie

"The only time I will leave here, will be when they take me to my resting place down the hill." he whispered.

Janie knew he meant St. John's Church in Buckhurst Hill. He had a fit of coughing, alarmed, she called the nurse who looked at Janie and sadly shook her head "not long now," she silently said; overcome with emotion and love for such a kind and gentle man. Touching her Grandfather gently, Janie whispered, "I love you". She turned away knowing she would never see him again. He passed away the next day with Grandma Annie by his side.

The powers to be took their time to bring home the

troops in Italy, for some were having the time of their lives it was said – drinking the wine, eating the food, seeing the sights. Though it was a bit farfetched. Besides where were the houses to house them, the furniture to fill them, and the jobs to maintain them? For at this time, over a thousand or more homes stood barely covered against the elements. Waiting for someone to repair them, for such materials were very short.

Finally, Arthur arrived home. Everyone was waiting to greet him, family-in-laws. Patsy had become very shy and hid behind Milly. Everyone listened to his words of wartime and funny events, which still happen even in wartime it seems.

One day, Arthur's wartime pals and their wives and girlfriends came to tea. There was much to talk about, laugh about and cry about. Twiggie, who had gone through as much with them, had been told he had but six months at the most to live. Tuberculosis; known as T.B. He had a lovely voice and was now singing to his wife.

"Mexsically Rose stop crying, I'll come back to you some sunny day. I'll be pining every hour that I'm away." Some such words, not a dry eye could be seen.

"Who's for tea or coffee?" asked Victoria

Chapter LIX

So peace time was very hard to adjust. And still over the other side of the world the major offensive was building up for the last big push. Then the H-bomb was dropped. The war on all fronts was coming to an end. The Second World War was over. What can one say about peace time? It was tough. Married sons and daughters still lived with their parents or in-laws including children. Rationing would be for many years. Hardly had the war ended, another started on the domestic front, what with high prices for old furniture; rents; houses and flats. The returning men were first on the governments list for houses. News Estates were being built outside the London area. Mr. Churchill's 'thousand 'ouses' a day had started. I believe he put his son-in-law in charge of reconstruction to make sure it would meet demands.

The house in Willow Grove Plaistow, had many upstairs rooms, so a little flat for Milly, Arthur and Patsy was put in place by Bill. This still left Victoria, Bill, Ted, George and Janie downstairs for eight months after the 'all clear'. No more convoys.

Still determined not to face another conveyor-belt in her life, Janie found a job in a government department. The mint, where old money was burnt and new notes printed in their thousands. Janie would have hundreds of thousands of these new smelling notes pass through her hands. She was looking for notes without numbers, so trays of money would be brought to the many long benches, where rows of women and girls sat silently facing each other. A stern looking women, one for each bench, sat on a high chair overlooking them all. Just in case one tucked a few into their bras or knickers thought Janie.

What chance, if any, for security was all around. Even the men shovelling the old notes into the furnaces had guards. What must they be thinking, money going up in flames and on pay day, five pounds to keep body and soul together, seemed to add insult to injury.

Many good times and laughter as returning family members from the services reached home. Uncle Charlie, home from the sea, had a girlfriend in America who was very keen on him. Her father had offered him a job in their firm if he wanted to stay. But he could not leave Grandma, alone. His mother needed all the help he could give her, but if she wanted to live in England, then they could be married. So on and off over the years, one or the other would cross the Atlantic Ocean. He never married; she did.

Sid returned from Egypt, blonde hair, bleached by the sun and tanned, was chased by the girls. Some were still left after the American withdrawal. So it wasn't long before he married. Milly, Victoria and Janie were having a cup of tea when a knock on the door had them looking at one another. Arthur was back on his beloved sea, and Jack working at the shipyard. The boys were at friend's houses. Victoria went downstairs to open it, the girls listening upstairs heard her say, "Well my word, Vincent, your back at last!" Milly looked at Janie, they could hear his footsteps on the stairs.
"I'll go and help Mum," she said. despite Janie's plea for her to stay. He greeted Milly on her way out and smiled at Janie. He hadn't changed, still as handsome as ever in his air force uniform.
"So good to see you Janie, and after all these years, still my old Janie I see." said Vincent. They were back on their old footing, the years between had gone.

Together they went dancing, with Billy Lane and his friend (who would become his wife). They went to the plays in the West End and to see the film 'The Third Man' starring James Mason. After this they went onto see his parents and brother at Frittenden. They walked through the forest as they had done during the war. It was while they were both laying the table, that Janie decided to put a question to him, that had been lying in her thoughts ever since the ending of the war. "Vincent, have you ever thought of living in Australia?" Without even turning round, his very firm answer was with a laugh,

"Oh no Janie, My country needs me!"

He was going back to finish his studies. Sadly, she turned away. She knew he loved her. Her thoughts turned to Frittenden, the lovely village in Kent, when he had taken their luggage and then all of them to Cherry Tree Farm in 1939; that lovely holiday. In one month war had been declared. The years he was in India and Burma they had kept in touch. Nine years they had known him. He was part of the family.

Why, why was the urge to go to Australia so strong? So many returned service men and women had found it hard to settle in Civy Street. Her job was a soulless one. Plenty of money lay within her reach, but not a penny was hers to spend; she laughed to herself, it had to be the right one, for this time there was no turning back. "Oh Donald!, why, why did you have to die?" sighed Janie.

At the crossroads again, which road to take...?

The End

Book Two

What Happened to Janie?

Janie was married at St John's Church Buckhurst Hill, Essex in 1947 to an airman she had met during the War. Vincent was best man. Coming out of the church Janie walked the short distance to Grandad's Holders grave and placing her bouquet of carnations and pinks on his grave, she said

"I love you Grandad"

The reception was held in the evening at the local hall. Sidney brought his dance band and sang many old wartime songs. Vincent requested a song and claimed Janie for the dance; it was 'No Souvenirs'. It goes:

"No Souvenirs for my treasure chest

By special request for no souvenirs

Don't give me one reminder

Don't give me one little thing

Nothing could be unkinder ..."

There certainly was something very special between Janie and Vincent. It left Janie wondering if the road she was now on was the right one. "Vincent resumed his studies and one day while playing rugby, he was knocked unconscious. They took him to emergency and he met a nurse there and married her. They had three sons. He became Principle of a college; he still visited the Reynolds over the years, but no Janie. Her husband Charles had joined the New Zealand Air Force; hence Janie and her two children Fran and Gerald moved to New Zealand.

New Zealand

She and her two small children boarded the Captain Cook in 1954. A few years had now passed since the war. Janie had met a man in the Air Force, Charles was his name. They decided to make a fresh start in New Zealand, so found themselves aboard a ship and now in the middle of a Typhoon. The captain's voice could be heard letting the passengers know yet again that the weather warning he had received yesterday was now upon them.

"All passengers must now clear the decks."

 Gerald, Janie's youngest child, took him at his word, he proceeded to push chair after chair through the ropes of the top deck, leaving them to be battered by the pounding sea. Stopping only at the appearance of his mother and sister who ordered he should cease such behaviour. He answered that he had the full backing of the captain. This amused Janie and her daughter Francesca.

The Typhoon was horrendous and Janie was using all her strength to hold on to her bunk, one of six in the cabin on the top deck, or was it the bottom. The ship was now in the eye of the storm it had turned day into night. Thunder and lightning, massive waves held the ship in a vice-like grip tossing it like a cork on water, to unbelievable heights and falling on one side or the other as the sea came crashing down. Smashing of china could be heard. Tables had been chained in the dining room for two days, were now desperate to break loose. A few hardy people still went for their meals, but most were flat on their backs or vomiting. This went on for days as the ship's captain and crew battled for survival. Janie, now lying in her bunk groaning, received little, if any help from the other occupants - nurses in the Royal New Zealand Air Force, for they were just as helpless as she.

The ship was full of young men and women from the war. Families tired of living in cramped houses waited for the call that never came for a house of their own. War tired, peace tired, they had answered the call from Australia and New Zealand, who needed them. The spirit of adventure had been dampened during the storm, but now all were on deck longing for land under their feet after five long weeks. So it was that Janie found herself in windy Wellington harbour, North Island. Now they must wait two days for a ferry to take half of the people on board to the South island. They had crossed from the North Pole to the South Pole, to the bottom of the world.

The hilly terrain in Wellington was a surprise, one had to board the small buses held by wires overhead and rails on the road as they screeched and groaned their way up one hill after another getting steeper and steeper. It was with a sigh of relief that one stepped off, but with the fear that one must return for there was no other way to the harbour that they knew of. Many boarding houses dotted the port, and the owners were used to the passengers from the other side of the world. But the sight of light snow on their houses and pavements sent them rushing in calling the children out to see it. But it was like taking coals to Newcastle for the children had come through a hard winter back in England. It was sunshine they wanted and plenty of it – but so near the South Pole? After all, Scott, the Arctic explorer had left from Christchurch, South island. So Janie had much ahead of her before Australia, the ships heading that way were always full.

It was a beautiful day when the ferry pulled in at Christchurch harbour. Port hills were all around, white painted houses with flowers on window boxes, in gardens, dotted the landscape. Sea gulls called their welcome landing on the ships rails and flying over the houses.

The UK men who had (after the war) joined the New Zealand armed forces, had gone on ahead of their wives and family, and were now waiting at the harbour to greet them. The nurses who had shared Janie's cabin had done the same and the transport was waiting to take them. Everyone had made friends over the weeks, now promised to keep in touch, although many of them had different paths to tread. Some had taken a two year contract to plant seedlings of trees, many to work on the farms.

Janie, eager to face her new way of life, was to find a very bumpy road ahead of her. Housing and rooms were in demand and high in price. Christchurch, a small town, with a church in the centre and shops with covers over the pavement to protect their stocks from fading. For the light this side of the world made one rush for sunglasses. The new comers stood out, for the local people were very casual in their dress. A few hotels did exist and she was grateful for she had lost her way and had walked longer than intended. No shops had been in sight and her thirst was awful. Pushing open the doors to the bar of one hotel, she could hardly see coming from the harsh light to the darkened room. At first she thought it was empty. Had she made a mistake? As her eyes adjusted to the room, she saw it was full of men, leaning on the bar counters, standing with glasses of beer, haze over their heads from cigarettes in hands and mouths. It was as if time had stopped for not a sound could be heard. The thirst driving her on Janie approached the bar. The woman behind the counter looked rough and tough. She stood eyeing Janie. "Please, a glass of lemonade or orange juice," she whispered. The woman seemed to hesitate, but gave it to her. Not a word had been uttered all this time. Janie downed the drink to the very last drop of the large glass. Cheers broke out from the men. The women sneered and said,

"You can tell what she is just by looking at her. I'm not supposed to serve the likes of you in here. It's men only, can't you read?" Later Janie found out it was 'swill hour'. Men rushed from their work into the bars to down as many pints as they could in the hour or so allowed by law. For all bars had to be closed very early in the evening.

"Welcome to my world!" for now Janie had come to conclusion she had stepped back fifty or more years in time.

Letters had arrived from home; all was well with Mum and Dad. Ted had been conscripted into the army and would no doubt be sent overseas. Milly and Arthur were now in one of Churchill's promised houses and were expecting another child. Grandma was not too well. Charlie had bought some land in Buckhurst Hill and had plans to build a cottage and have a small piggery as a hobby. Uncle Max had passed away. Brenda had gone back to her Mansion in the country. George and his wife Vera had also moved into a new house a week ago. Vincent was now out of studies and teaching in a college. He had visited once or twice. The last time he had brought home a nurse. It appears he had been knocked unconscious while playing rugby and she was the nurse who attended him. A very nice person, Victoria wrote. They did marry and in years to come had three boys.

New Zealand is called 'the land of the long white cloud'. The North Island has in parts a volcanic structure and is well known for its hot springs. A journey by ferry got one from the North to the South Island, which is situated closer to the South Pole, a lot colder and greener. Christchurch, nestled at the foot of the Port Hills would become Janie's home for many years and she would give birth to five more children. Christchurch was a beautiful city. The Avon River meandered through the town. Weeping willows dipped their branches into the cool clear water that sparkled in the sunlight giving the impression of extreme placidity. Janie sat down on the grass. Taking off her shoes, she sighed with relief as her burning feet, touched the cool water. She looked around, not a person in sight, just the odd car passing.

Having walked through many parks, one, she thought, could be forgiven for believing they were back home, for it was as English as any county town. The early settlers had done their best to make it so. Yet it had rebelled in its colonial streets. Buildings hastily put up structures some more like large sheds, in contrast to the beautiful buildings constructed by convict labour. How hard it must have been to have been deported for stealing a loaf of bread through hunger, or poaching a rabbit. Torn from family and sent in ships over crowded both in humans and rats which had the freedom of the ships. Not so the humans locked in the ship's bowels, not knowing if it was day or night, water leaking constantly in their ears and wondering what hell may lay ahead. What deprivation, what humiliation, what triumph if they could again be free.

There stood the church, its steeple pointing to heaven. It stood in the town's centre, the stained glass windows shedding some outside light to its darkened interior leaving a somewhat eeriness by the colours reflecting on benches and walls. The wooden beams still emanated the smell of the forest mixed with the musty smell of death for here lay the first Bishop of Canterbury in his stone coffin.

Coming out into daylight, Janie crossed the square to a group of shops. One had odds and ends of everything. She went inside to browse. Men were bringing some paintings in and standing them side by side. There were about six and those facing her were the chiefs of the Maori in all their war paint, fierce looking, hair plaited or piled high with a feather, no doubt making some statement as to what tribe they were head of. Later she was to read, they were cannibals and would fight over the heart of a brave enemy, which they thought could bring his strength into them. For they were fierce fighters and today she noticed they were gentle but firm, though the women she found were rather superstitious. But one way or the other we all have that trait in us no matter how small.

Women's clothes in the stores were somewhat out of date. The women would stop a new arrival asking about the dress or costume and enquiring about some place they or their parents had come from back home. People were very friendly.

So time passed as it always does. She was homesick and longed to return to 'dear old' England, yet knew that in the years that had passed that 'dear old' England would have changed. Opening up the morning paper she saw a picture of Vincent. He was helping a farmer dig his sheep out of the heavy snow in Frittenden. What memories that name and place bought to her mind. The happy holidays of yester-years.... the time before the war. Yes, he would be there, for his mother and father had lived all their lives in that lovely village. She hoped all had gone well with him and his family.

Janie and Charles had met here and there at odd times and now had been married many years for seven children had been born to them. Her husband had left the air force after two years and now worked in an office in the city. They had bought a house sometime ago in one of the suburbs. Some of the children were now at college. Bringing up four boys and three girls was a tall order even in such a country as New Zealand with its fresh food and fish. But it had taken Janie sometime to come to terms with the way meat was sold. After the very little they lived on during the war, people here would eat a great deal of meat because it was at this time so cheap, so whole sides of meat – lamb, mutton would be bought.

One day, Janie saw a bicycle parked outside a shop had a shoulder of mutton tied to the carrier at the back of the bike. The paper had been torn and dozens of blue bottles were having a great time. It was sometime before she could even look into a window of a meat shop.

Wide open places, outdoor events. The beaches had lots of people and stones. Tides could be strong, underwater rips could pull people out in seconds. So much danger to lives and at times the waters would hold the very dangerous blue bottle jellyfish. So long as people knew of these things and stayed clear at these times, great fishing, sports, horse-riding, camping. Schools were run on the English timetable. Colleges private were mostly all boys or all girls.

Needing extra cash as most parents do, she answered an advert for a few hours work she could fit it in while the children were at school. She walked to the college. The priest in charge of such matters was very keen for her to start work right away. Of course they could not afford the rates of pay she would receive outside, but this was a church college. Whose fees were very high she thought, for her eldest son attended there. She accepted the rate and was shown what to do by the woman in charge. Come meal time, she was to stand at the long table for the brothers, mostly teachers at the college. The other women had the lecturers at her table. The tables were beautifully laid, each brother had their own serviette ring to hold their table napkin. Some she noticed were pure silver. In they came and sat down. She served the soup, collected the dishes.

    All went well at her job for a few weeks. She had noticed a very old priest who sat at the top of her table and sometimes spilled his soup as old people do for his hands shook. Making sure his table napkin, which was very large covered his long gown as much as possible, she did her best for him. She also noticed the young brothers looked at him and laughed amongst themselves. She questioned the other women who told her the old priest had been one of the first to teach at the college and had, in his time, written many books but refused to be sent away to an old priest home. Later going to a very old wash house to collect a broom, she found him in his wheelchair. The place was gloomy, grimy, the habitat of a few rats. Had a person put him there or had he hidden himself away from the world. Still the tittering went on amongst the young brothers (yes one day you'll be old, that's for sure!). The lectures, she noticed, passed their plates after each course along the line to the top of the table. This enabled the woman to serve the next one quickly, thereby finishing before Janie.

One of the teachers she noticed had a lot to say for himself and was looked up to by some of the others. The pure silver engraved crested serviette ring. So one day she asked them would they please help her by passing the plates as the others did on the next table. Indignation crossed his face as he told the others it was her job and she should do it. All were listening on the next table. She looked at them all. "Where's your Christianity, brothers?" said Janie. Laughter broke out on the next table, as one by one the brothers left the table, not waiting for the meal to continue.

Janie went to the priest in charge to hand her notice in. "No don't leave," he implored. "Look, we need help in the meals quarter for the boarders." It was after school hours but she agreed, for the eldest children would look after the younger ones for a few hours.

It was a different part of the college that she entered through the kitchen. The scene before her was one of utter chaos. A man about forty years of age was staggering about the room that was so filthy as to make her reach for her handkerchief. A huge slab of margarine lay on the dirty floor with lumps of coal embedded in it. It was hard to walk through the rotting vegetables cardboard boxes and dust bin overloaded, spilt on the floor. The drunken man had brought out huge trays of fatty mutton chops which he slopped into unclean frying pans. Huge pots of cabbage, which had turned a nasty grey colour and potatoes over cooked. She turned the gas off before leaving for the dining hall. The boys sat at bare tables, having queued for their meals were dished into army pans. Before long the almost full pans were placed on the counter ready to be disposed of into the piggery. The college had a farm of sorts. This went on night after night.

Two boys were placing their army pans on the counter. "You can't be hungry boys"

"We can't eat that muck," said one boy. "We spend all our pocket money sent to us on food at the shops." Janie was ready to go home when the matron walked in. Janie pointed to the pig bins, "They live it up," she said. "Well the boys will spend their pocket money on food."

"Does that mean they are too well fed?"

"My boys have baked beans on toast now and then. It might do these lads a least one night a week." Matron looked shocked. But she agreed to give it ago next evening as the chef wasn't feeling too well. Now it was the turn of the boys to be shocked. Huge cans of baked beans were opened and dozens of loaves of bread were toasted. They came back for more. No waste this evening. Matron came to see how it was all going. Instead she looked at the empty pig bins.

"Oh, our poor pigs will have to go without, this is terrible."

"But the boys loved it for a change," said Janie. The pigs never had to miss a meal after that.

"I'll never understand why the lads eat as they do, yet the brothers and priest dine so well. The tables should be laid as theirs are. One brother or priest should sit at the head of each table. It's my opinion that etiquette is every bit as important in the world as learning." Her words fell on deaf ears. It was all too much for them. Janie sighed. She still thought she had stepped back in time.

She had got over her surprise of seeing children from a Catholic and state school walk on different sides of the road, when on their way home, calling each other names and throwing stones. It may have been confined to this little town by the sea, but it smacked of the dark ages.

"Winging pom" was often openly said to one's face. Pom would be noted if not stated. Pom meant 'Prisoner of her Majesty' which puzzled Janie, for most earlier settlers were just that. Perhaps in the years to come they will be proud of their heritage. Her children were proud to be New Zealanders. So one was welcome in one way, but not quite accepted.

One man told her, "I'll never understand. I've been in this country sixty years and still remain a pom. Others coming in from other lands are called New Zettlers. Britten has poured millions into building Australia up and still we are poms over there."

"Just be proud of it, I know I am," said Janie.

The earth quake struck early in the morning. Down came the books from the shelves. China from the dresser crashed on to the floor. The house shook. The family hung on to whatever was close to them. It was their first since arriving in New Zealand. Many times they had heard that New Zealand was fast sinking under the sea. Many landslides near the coasts and houses falling into the sea, no doubt due to the very strong pull of the tides. Huge rocks had been brought into the coastal areas to combat mother-nature. Little could be done about the earthquakes; they just came and had to be dealt with.

No one was hurt, more of course would come. Japan or Indonesia had them, then somehow the fault line would be affected in parts of the world and New Zealand had many fault lines running through it. Oh well, little could be done about it. So it will no doubt be forgotten until next time. The day just continued as it always does, hardly anyone mentioned it.

Hamner Springs was well known for its hot springs. Sulphur, one was warned not to put their head under water for fear of meningitis. The family had been there for a holiday. The mountains loomed high and looked so close when one opened the window of the lodge house called the Cuckoo's Nest (strange but true). Was I disappointed at all? (It well and truly lived up to all expectations.) One house was built in the shape of a UFO on stilts. Nelson, a place somewhat like Kent in England, the soil was marvellous for growing most vegetables and fruits and at this time isolated
.

A Strange turn of Events

Janie had another encounter with a UFO. One day taking a bus into the city, a silver-shaped oblong UFO kept pace and on level with the bus. One could not see inside it, for not a window could be seen. The passengers were terrified and a lady on the bus couldn't stop screaming. The driver had become nervous and built up speed, and our bus was swerving all over the road, until he finally decided to pull in, the UFO then departed as quickly as it came. There were reported sightings all over the city of Christchurch that day. Members of the public reported seeing it on the outskirts of the city and that it took off with such speed that made one think it was a delusion.

Many times during the war, the boys flying their planes had seen many such objects but 'hush hush' had been demanded from the high ranks and stamped confidential. Sometimes it was hard to come to terms with the unknown. Not only was

Janie witness to UFO sightings, but also the house she moved into was haunted. It was a large house with many windows and had been built on a reclaimed riverbed. It was so damp inside that shoes in cupboards would turn green with mildew. Many houses had been built on this land, which should not have passed for building. The top end of the street was dry compared with the lower end, for every winter it was flooded.

Yet this was not all, for not long after Janie and her family moved in, did they discover that something had moved in before us. At certain times, mostly in the evening, about the time the children were in bed would come the sound of heavy old fashion shoes 'clip-clopping' around the house at night, and then would come the digging of a heavy spade against gravel. This went on incessantly, night after night for years. They had a ghost that was for sure.

The girls in their bedrooms would hide under the bed clothes if still awake. The boys went out armed with hammers and axes to investigate but found nothing. 'The Styx' that ran parallel to our house is the river that leads to the underworld.
It was such a golden moonlit night, the red glow spread over the house, trees and fields. Tired Janie was glad to climb into bed and drifted off to sleep only to be woken up by screams and sounds of struggles on her doorstep. Looking out of her bedroom window she looked to the front door. Muddy footsteps could be seen which could have been left by anyone she thought. Climbing back into bed again, she was woken up by someone shaking her.

A woman dressed in old fashioned clothes stood beside her bed. The glow from the blood moon showed the distress she was in. She wanted Janie to know. She was on her way to meet the man she loved. She was leaving her drunken husband, her two children she had left with her mother and she would send for them. As she was crossing the stony riverbed, her husband had attacked and murdered her. Her distress was for her children who must think she had left them. Sadly Janie watched her leave. The footsteps ceased, much to the relief of the children. What dark secrets did that river hold to be so named? One year later another woman was found with her throat cut, replenishing the dark river.

The dampness of the house now compelled the family to move out for health reasons. I was relieved in a way for she felt and always had done, that it had been a big mistake to have moved there in the first place. It was her husband's choice and she had gone along with it. There had been happy times for the children who loved their play hut built into a tree top despite the bull who sometimes stood underneath them.

They moved to a place called Leithfield, about twenty miles out of Christchurch to an old cottage on two acres of land opposite a school. Leithfield a tiny village, comprised of a scattering of houses a local store, school, one pub, land, trees and winding lanes. A few buses a day would connect people to the city, which was expanding with the influx of immigrants. They grew all their vegetables, planted fruit trees, kept bees, kept chickens, a few sheep and a calf.

Janie's connection with the other side was not over, for one morning on waking Janie heard the most glorious singing. It brought back memories of the Welsh Choir she had heard over the radio in England. She had not seen or heard of a church. So where were the people?

The children complained she was tucking them in too tightly at night while they slept, for they were unable to move.

Now Janie herself was tucked in and she understood why, it was indeed hard to move. At night she would feel a wavering motion of her bed blanket as if she were rising and falling, this was the ghost tucking her in.

Janie decided to investigate the history of Leithfield for any clues as to the origins of this ghost. Looking at an old map of the district she found a church had at one time stood on the now vacant piece of land opposite their cottage. The kindly old soul tucking them in was a Nun. Although getting out of bed every morning was difficult, no one minded this ghost as she was nurturing.

Some funny things would happen to Janie in this secluded village. Today she needed some items from the shop down the lane, so down she walked. "Taking the family for a walk?" asked an old man. She stopped for a few words and then moved on. "Where's your flute?" said another. Puzzled, Janie looked behind her and saw the chickens, the sheep, the calf and a few ducks all moving when she moved and stopping when she did. Waiting till a bend in the road enabled her to turn and head back in the direction they had come from.

Victoria, Bill, Doris (Victoria's youngest sister) and her husband arrived after five weeks on the ship. Ted and Janie were pleased to see them. Janie introduced them to the grandchildren they had never seen. James had two of his own born in New Zealand, now making four.

"Everything is so behind the times," Victoria said. "How ever did you put up with it Janie all these years?"

"I had very little choice Mum once the children came along,"

But she knew it was very hard for them to adjust to this way of life. It was easy going than the ways of London, in dress and manners. Then Bill's health took a turn for the worst. They had been here in New Zealand for two years. They had made friends (as was their way), loved all their grandchildren and had planned a return trip to London to see Milly and George. One day while out with Victoria, Bill found he was fighting to breath. He was rushed to hospital and the medical results showed he had lung cancer. At first they said he had but two weeks to live. They didn't know Bill! With medical help he lived two years.

"He was never happy here Mum. He should not have come!" said Janie.

"But we did and it's a lovely country, let's not look back." replied Victoria

Victoria was to return to London many times in the years that passed. Then one time she did not return. She became ill. She was about eighty one years when she passed away. Poor Bill died at sixty five years, after all his hard work. Some of the jobs might have brought on the cancer, asbestos in the building of houses, gasworks. He did not live long enough to claim his pension. Victoria's ashes were sent to New Zealand and buried beside Bill's.

Janie's own family were growing up. Her eldest daughter, Francesca, moved to Australia, the eldest son ,Gerald now out of college, joined the army. The third son, Kevin, had gone to join his sister in Australia and had gone back packing around the world at the tender age of sixteen. "Too many Biggles books," Charles said. Still Janie feared for him. He could have written books on what he saw and went through.

Six years later he returned. Janie's other four children were still at school, Nigel, Michael, Theresa and Dolores.

Australia

 Janie, Bert, Theresa and Dolores, looked down on Sydney Australia as the plane came in to land. Her eldest daughter had invited them over during the holidays. She had just rented a house in the North Shore and had plenty of room. The house was set in a deep dip and was covered with overgrown bushes. It was the time of the year when the dreaded funnel web spiders, usually in their hundreds, would come from under roots of trees and bushes. They had a love of damp places. They were often found in houses, on swings in the garden and sheds. Some people had died from their bites, for they would jump at you if one went on the attack. One had half an hour to seek help it was said, for as yet, no antidote had been found in the seventies (but no doubt would be). It was surprising considering the population, the deaths were small.

 The house situated in the suburb of Artarmon in the lower North Shore of Sydney, was dark and gloomy inside, immediately Janie could sense there was something terribly wrong about the house. She felt a very dark presence. Looking round, Janie noticed the painted walls showed bad taste in décor, more so in the bathroom – no window and painted a very dark green. Her daughter, reading her thoughts said, "It's all I could get Mum." High rents meant few houses or flats, so much so, that some owners did not bother to have them cleaned. So were left with dirty ovens, floors and partly furnished, soiled mattresses. So all in all, her daughter was lucky – or was she!

They woke up tired and extremely drained the next morning, but shrugged it off, putting it down to the heat of the day (much hotter than NZ). It was mainly at night that strange things occurred. The radio would blare, lights turned on and off and doors slammed the record player would start up and turned up to full capacity music would boom out loud enough to wake up the whole neighbourhood. The daughter said she had been aware of the ghost, but that it was acting up when she had people over to stay. A few nights of this found them sleeping on mattresses in one room. Janie called a Priest who brought holy water and a large cross, they opened all the windows and he sprinkled holy water in every room. Someone put garlic in all the rooms and prayers were said for the lost soul whoever he or she was. The Priest soon bolted white as a sheet from the house as the Poltergeist was so outraged at the holy man, that he began to throw things around the room only just missing the Priests head. So that didn't work. Janie let the sun into the house by putting up the blinds and cutting the overgrown bushes. Whatever it was it resented her she felt. After the incident with the Priest, the ghost became more active and bold. No one was keen to have a bath and kept some underwear on under the shower, for fear of being watched.

Her son Kevin was also due to visit Francesca in Sydney. One day with a knock on the door, there stood the backpacker son who had been travelling the world since he was sixteen. Looking older for he was now twenty two years and very tired from his long journey. They were delighted to see him after all these years. Looking at his sisters he remarked how grown up they looked, as if it had suddenly dawned on him how long he had been away. They all sat listening to his tales of some of his exploits, but could see how tired he was. He said good night and went into a back bedroom.

A storm after the heat of the day had started so when the sliding door began to open and shut and the French doors leading to the garden burst open, letting the torrential rain in. After getting up many times he tied the handles on the French doors. Perhaps now he could get some sleep.

Little did he know what he was up against, for the poltergeist would not stop until he left. The room became cold, so cold it was impossible to sleep. Getting up, he put more covers on the bed. Now it would be warmer he thought. Until they were ripped off with such violence as to send him in terror to join the girls in their room on the floor shivering with the cold. They put bedclothes on him, but could he sleep? Next morning he told them all they could not possibly live in such a house. He still had a week before his flight to NZ and would help them look for quieter lodgings, which they found much to the relief of all.

Janie helped her daughter with the moving. One day while Janie was packing her daughters household goods, when the house alarm started ringing. It was not long after that, that the beaded curtains in the hall were torn down. Janie tried to make a run for it, but this creature blocked her path. A young man, curly hair, laughing, his evil face was taunting her, daring her to move. Staring him in the face she stood her ground. She knew now a terrible thing he had done, this was the day they had taken him away two years ago from murdering his sister. The door bell rang. She opened the door, the police stood there. "Your house alarm, would you like us to turn it off? Your next door neighbour rang us." Gratefully she said yes please. Many years later, one of her daughters went back to look at the house; there it stood deep in its hollow far below the street level, surrounded by bushes, painted black all over with its blinds down against the world. "It was horrifying," she said. The poltergeist was still in control.

Janie and her family soon after moved permanently to Australia. Sydney with its Harbour Bridge and opera house, its sprawling city, had much to offer. Plenty of jobs and good pay Plenty of shops, cafes, hotels, good transport, entertainment and plenty of adventure in its vast outback. Schools in her opinion were not up to the standard in NZ. Trains were full to capacity which reminded her of London in peak hour.

The dreaded funnel web spiders, snakes, for many times one would be crossing a road with a large snake more so in the hilly North Shore. If a window was left open a very large carpet snake would go in and take a look around. Bird life was beautiful and still is. Plenty of libraries – a huge one in Martin Place, centre of the city. Janie loved to get lost in such places.

Janie's children were all growing up. Her eldest daughter, Francesca, had taken to the stage singing and dancing. The eldest son, Gerald, had a very high IQ and was now drafted into the army as they must and loved it. The second son, Kevin, had just arrived back from his years of travel. The third son, Nigel, loved the farm, but had a great talent in almost anything he wanted to do. Her fourth son, Michael, – well it's a miracle he's still here; one and a half pounds at birth. He was very talented could sing and play the guitar. The second daughter, Theresa, she recalled, taking her to her first day of school – she sat down on the mat (they all had mats) looked at her teacher and never since looked up from a book. Her youngest daughter, Dolores, had a talent for art.

Janie missed the small township of Christchurch, which reminded her of England, but not its narrow mindedness of yesterday years. Some day she would return to London to see Milly and George, who were very happy with their lot, so to speak. George and his wife had a great deal to do with the scout movement, sports, archery, canoeing, camping and watched many of the boys grow up and was proud of them as of his own two sons.

His wife also loved her garden and Janie received videos of many happy times, with Milly, Arthur and their three daughters, reminding Janie of the sing songs before and during the war and after war until she went overseas. Yes the family loved to sing. Ted had and perhaps still has a great voice. "It's music for the soul," Granddad would say. Janie's family loved to sing and the teachers at school would send them from class to class to sing the songs they had composed themselves.

Time changes many things. Arthur had met with an accident on his way to work and hovered between life and death. Milly sat by his side day and night, sometimes he would mutter yellow car. The police man took one look at him and shook his head. Arthur had been in all the tough battles in the war and his biggest battle to survive was in his hands. He did survive though battered, bruised and full of tin plates in his legs and in parts of his body. On walking he had sticks, drove the car, played the Uke, sang his songs and told his naughty jokes. Milly saw the yellow car. Yes Milly found that outside the police station. "That's the car that ran my husband down," she said. She could have add and change his life forever for he never complained of his pain.

Ted and his wife Peggy were staying with Milly and Arthur. A number of years later Arthur had gone on his usual hospital check up. He had a massive heart attack. Milly must have been grateful to have her two brothers beside her daughters at her side in such sad times. But we see him still happy as ever with his family around him on the videos. That's how we all remember him. How they must miss him. Time waits for no man, the sun rises and sets today becomes yesterday and years roll by. Uncle Charlie and Sid passed away in their forties, a great surprise for all.

Janie enjoyed her travelling, this time into the outback with her son, who owned an old beat up car. The odd store could be found after miles of shrubs, bushes dry land and kangaroos. Calling into one such place, he parked his car and entered the broken down old office shop. "I see you have a Holden." he nodded, "What is it Holden in boy bolts." Ha ha ha. Out back humour, tell us about it. The next stop was shed like, selling petrol, a few beers, tea-cakes, that sort of thing. Rusty drums, run down ram shacked, a number of hot dusty travellers hanging around waiting to be served.

Janie was chatting to the owner who was complaining about having to do everything. His wife he said went out a few days ago and left him to do it all. There was muttering of sympathy. "Isn't it just like a sheila," said one.

"Never trust them," muttered another, while they shuffled from one foot to another longing to get back on the road, yet having to wait for petrol. "Mind if I fill up mate?""She'll be right, sorry for the hold up."

Janie and her son, with the car now filled up with petrol, went back on the road. Janie mentioned to her son that she felt some kind of presence in the shop and saw the ghost of a woman. Picking up a newspaper sometime later they saw a picture of the place. All the time the missing wife was dumped into a drum not far away. The alarm bells had been raised.

"Why would he do such a thing mum?" Kevin asked Janie. "Sun stroke perhaps" Janie replied.

Janie was to be a witness of many more sightings of UFOs as the years went by. She was on a bus travelling across the Nullarbor desert, when she sighted a couple of orange balls in the sky dancing around one another and then quickly disappeared before she could raise the alarm. More and more dreams of future events, in great detail came and went, always that fear of not being believed, held her back for she had suffered cruelly in the past for her beliefs.

Tasmania

Janie briefly took up residence at her son's farm in Tasmania. . Her travelling son had decided to settle down. He had bought this farm in Richmond, Tasmania and put a lovely stone cottage on a high part of a hill and planted about two thousand native trees in the front and both sides. At the back there were native bushes and a small river that had flowed for many years. It was an ideal place to have a picnic or rest your feet in its cool waters. A track from the village ran along the river but was little used, if ever by other people.

One night in the cottage, Janie lay half asleep, she felt the temperature in the room suddenly drop by about ten degrees. Janie turned her head towards the door, where she saw a man and a woman in a grey like mist. In a much lighter mist three children, the eldest first, then the next youngest last. Round to her side of the bed they came. They stood looking down at her as she looked up at them. The man and woman were dressed alike in what seemed to be a greyish uniform, more like a tunic with a whitish round collar. The hair on their heads was very closely cropped, high cheek bones, eyes large, but not overly large. Not too sure, she could see his mouth but knew it was there. He knew she could see him. He said something to the woman as if telling her, she could see him. She also looked down. He turned his head towards the woman and Janie also looked at her. These visitors from another dimension or perhaps a different part of the Universe seemed to know Janie. She had felt a fondness from them towards her. Then she felt herself drift off to sleep.

She woke up next morning almost frozen, so cold as if she had been in a refrigerator, not able to move could hardly speak. When she could she said to Charles, "Am I as cold as I feel?" He touched "my god it is like you have been put into a refrigerator. This family would come many times. Each time it was the same – looking around the cottage not a thing had been touched. Locks still on the doors, windows latched. She had never felt fear for they seemed gentle and had a firm order of discipline and respect for each other that she came to admire. These people were different from those she had seen as a child. They had been tall with helmets which they could remove once inside the spaceship. Could there be more?

The Port Arthur Killer

Janie was planting tomatoes and corn in a low part of the field on the farm in Richmond. She suddenly felt very uneasy, looking up from her planting, Janie saw a blonde headed young man standing in amongst the trees watching her. A sick feeling past through her and she had a vision of blood splattered across the fields. Janie felt so nauseous and frightened that she quickly retired indoors. Although on their property, he made no attempt to speak or move. She looked back at the cottage some distance away – he had disappeared. With some trepidation, she continued her work as if he was not there although she still felt him watching her. Day by day he appeared as if he were an apparition. Until one evening, a shadow fell across the lounge room and standing outside on the veranda looking in at herself (Charles was watching TV) was this person. He made no move until she approached the sliding doors and again he was off. Her son and his wife and family lived in the village. He came several times to work on the farm but could not see the intruder. On and off he would hang around, though rather reluctantly to go down, she went to gather her produce and plant.

One day, Charles was working by the river. It was time for lunch, so started to make his way back unaware he was being followed by this person, who disappeared amongst the trees. Janie was watching the scene before her. What could they do? Not much, but he gave her the creeps. Her sons came round many times and gave her a dog and fitted an alarm. So things improved, the dog would chase him off. Once Janie saw his photo in the paper and what he did at Port Arthur on TV. She foresaw that it could have been them held up in their cottage, instead of the elderly couple who died at his hands, with all those innocent people, for Richmond was on his list. It was reported he killed thirty five people and injured at least twenty more at Port Arthur, a town not far off far Richmond. To her he will always remain the silent assassin, for in all that time he never uttered a word. The farm was eventually sold.

Janie became a Clairvoyant

By now Janie had gained a reputation as a psychic. She had at first looked into the hands of people just to pass the time away at a gathering, just for fun. Then more people came, for the visions she saw and spoke about came true. People started to come to her in droves, as word of mouth went around, wanting to know about their health, money, business. CEOs of large corporations would come to discuss what moves they should make and what would the outcome be. Love and travel loomed large in the young as it still does. Most people she met were very nice, some brought chocolates, flowers, crystals, tapes of them singing and books they had written. Many returned time and time again. Then the demand came to travel from place to place, city to city, talks on radio and TV appearances, newspaper reporters, magazine articles, but not a word would Janie tell of her dreams of future events.

Not until the Mount Erebus disaster. She read in the paper that the pilot was to blame. This she knew was wrong for three weeks earlier she had been on board the plane in her dreams. The people on board were happy, laughing, drinking champagne. She had made her way unnoticed to the front of the plane and stood beside the pilots. The horror and surprise in their faces, she'll never forget. As a mountain loomed in front of them, too late for action of any kind, the plane crashed into it. She had woken from her dreams upset. She knew the impending disaster was in a mountain region. Where? She hadn't been told. But she knew now that the Mount Erebus disaster was the one she had witnessed in her dreams. She wrote straight away to a New York paper and a New Zealand one. The flight had left from there. Thank goodness she was believed and it was taken up. She had not put her name or address. The same old fear still bugged her. The pilots name was cleared. It was reported something about the wrong flight path.

She was certain her dreams came from the unknown, may be another dimension, showing her these incidents may be to prevent them from happening. But who would believe her?
Then there were the dreams about the Mountbatten murders. Janie at this time was now living in Perth, Western Australia. Every detail had been shown to her in her dreams for many times the dream returned. Lord Mountbatten had featured many times in World War II. He was a strong leader of men, a Navy Commander.

The other day on TV Janie heard a person say, "No one knows future events," a very broad statement, with a very limited outlook. Janie was in high demand with her psychic abilities and often spent her time reading people's palms. One day, a gentleman accompanied his wife to a reading, while reading his wife's hand she looked up and asked the husband, "Have you still got your tape measure in your pocket?" Surprised, he produced it. She also provided descriptions and the gender of two of his grandchildren yet to be born. A house they would buy and (a boat half in, half out of the water – people with life jackets on and a very loud explosion, no one will be hurt.) five years later that did happen. This couple were one of many people who Janie could assist with her psychic abilities. While Janie was on talk- back radio, a man phoned in to ask a question. She felt concerned for him. She asked him to come to see her. She was right to be concerned for the vision came. He was surrounded by police. Stay away from trouble she pleaded and don't wear black (unlucky for him) for the consequences will be dire if you dismiss my advice, for other people were involved. He said later to his wife he wished he had listened, for himself and others were on charges of murder.

It was not all gloom as she reported many happy events, lucky numbers, and all sorts of good things. Janie saw a tumour behind the eye of a woman's young daughter. The woman came back and said she had taken her daughter to have her eyes tested. No, no said Janie, she must see an eye specialist. She did and he operated and saved her sight. Good outcome.

Janie saw so many events, too many to record. A scientist from a university (one of many) came with his wife. "We have been looking for a house to buy, but no success."
 "You have been looking in the wrong direction. Now go in the opposite direction. You will find the house next to a small business." They later informed her that they had found it and bought it.

 By now, Janie strongly believed that some events were laid down years ahead, but could be altered to a certain extent by the actions (free will or decisions taken unbeknownst of what lay ahead.) by a person. She came to realize that positive thinking in a person's life was so very important – as she could see the dark negative energy surround people with depression. One had to work on a lot on self development and find contentment in things such as, singing, painting, dancing or any sort of creative activity. Taking a day at a time, dwelling on good times, not bad, one should learn from bad times, become stronger. Goodness knows Janie had encountered many such times and learnt from them as we all must.

 But as we near the end of Janie's story, she will continue to relate the important cases and people that came into her life, but only some of them for it had been a long tale to tell, but a true one. Take the Lindy Chamberlain case. At first

Janie took little interest in it, but most of the country did, so much so, as the case continued people would end up brawling over the outcome. Was she guilty or not guilty? It turned this way and that. Did the dingo take her baby? What was it about Lindy Chamberlain that made one like or dislike her so much? After a while, listening to what evidence came to light, Janie was convinced she was innocent. The more she thought on it, the more the dreams came. She left a note at one of the news stations stating her beliefs. Spoke over the air, but she needed some kind of proof, as the trial dragged on. Many people related to the case came to see her. She recognised one person who was a witness in the case. Janie's visions and dreams about the Lindy Chamberlin case continued. Janie now firmly believed that she was innocent, but unfortunately, she was found guilty. The reporter on the case was in Janie's opinion good at his work. There was a mention by Lindy of a missing baby jacket but few people believed her. Until Janie saw the jacket lying in mud, in her dream, at what looked like the bottom of a hill.

    Janie rang the reporter. Yes, she told him there was a baby's jacket; it had a pattern on it, and was covered in mud. Sometime later the jacket was found and had been covered in mud. If only she had known where to look for it. It was somewhere in the outback. She knew nothing of the place. Janie was pleased to see Lindy Chamberlain finally released from prison.

    For many weeks Janie and some of her family had been on the road travelling from Sydney to Perth. What an adventure the Nullarbor Plain proved to be. Janie's son, Kevin, took a side turning from the main road having driven most of the day and evening was now upon them. The lane was long and winding coming to an end by a watering hole for horses in days long gone. A few tents dotted the landscape. The owners looked up from their seats outside.

"Travelled far mate?"
"Sure have, too far for one day. Can one get food around here?"
"Nope, all closed for the day."
"Want a hand with that tent?"
"Thanks mate."

Before long they were warm and cosy in their sleeping bags. Janie was a short distance from the tent's entrance. It must have been two or three o'clock in the morning when she was roughly shaken.

"Come on Jack, put your great coat on, it's cold outside. We have got to hit the road."

Janie could hear the snorting of the horses and their hooves pawing the gravel. Janie looked outside the tent to see what the commotion was all about, but when she popped her head out, there was no one in sight and all was quiet again.

The next morning they headed towards a village. The smell of freshly baked bread reminded them all of the hunger they felt. So they followed the road to the village of Rutherglen. Still eating their hot rolls, they wandered from place to place and there before their eyes were everything one could wish for about Ned Kelly, his letters regarding the police and their treatment of him. He wrote very well and with feeling. In the not too far distance stood two old fashioned chimney stacks, rebelling against time, nothing but the dried up grass and the sky above. "That's the remains of Ned Kelly's house" someone said.

Janie knew it must have been Ned Kelly who had woken her but still uncertain as to who this Jack was. So his ghost and not doubt some of his gang must still roam the area. But that's what Ned Kelly is all about isn't it? And Ned wouldn't have it any other way, for she still remembers his persistent shaking to wake her. Janie wanted to linger to find out all she could in this intriguing place with so much information. Instead she settled for some souvenirs and found to her delight a small dish made in Britain. Imprinted on it was, "The old Curiosity shop" which brought Victorians to their knees in abject sorrow over little Nell. Can anyone forgive Charles Dickens for letting her die? Her daughter in law insisted on buying it for her, knowing Janie's love of Dickens books. It is much treasured.

By now Janie had come to terms with her way of life. She was able to tell fishermen where they would find the biggest catch. People looking for sunken treasure were given a fair idea where to look, once she had seen the map. Janie dreamt of the spies on board the American Navy ship. They did find them. The Chinese man who had written on paper so long that he put it on a wall in China. A month later there he was on TV doing just that. What he had written, she had no idea. Why the dream?

Two people came to see her. One was a woman who was very homely and kind, accompanied by her very short husband. Janie saw the husband first. "Please look in my hand and tell me what you see," he asked. Janie could see that he had worked for the English government which was confirmed by him. She told him there would be a court case over a book he had written; he asked her if he would win the case? She told him he would be successful. 'The Spy Catcher' the author was 'Peter Wright'. Margaret Thatcher, the Prime minister of England was trying to stop the publication in Australia – which only helped to sell the book. Janie bought one. She thought what a lovely couple they were. His words as he left, "How could you know so much about me?" She also had asked herself that question many times without coming up with an answer.

Janie was often traumatised by her dreams of the future, as it was hard to get anyone to believe her. So Janie often remained silenced when it came to her dreams. One day the phone rang and Janie answered it. It was a reporter from a newspaper. "I just had to phone you," she said, "have you anything to tell Madam Janie?" Just at that moment the Space Shuttle Challenger exploded before her eyes in a vision. Janie knew the Alien Connection had given her a warning of what was to come and they had wanted her to tell the reporter. She had many dreams on the Challenger telling her things were not going well, and the material they used was not up to standard – too thin and not of worthy space travel. The Challenger was due to take off in a few days, but who would have listened to her? Being a Clairvoyant, she did not have a hot line to NASA She hoped the flash she had received was not true. Sadly her fear were realized when the Challenger did indeed explode on its way up. How sad it was for all involved.

What now? What next?

She had for a long time traversed memory lane. Indulged in past loves, shed tears amongst laughter, now my story has come to an end. She always lived by her father's morals and wisdom:

"The truth Janie, always tell the truth."

Janie did visit England in 1982 ,1987 & 2013 Bamfords store is now demolished. Bogner Reges cottage has long gone. She did not visit Frittenden in Kent - that village of many happy memories.

The Current Age of the Reynolds family:
Milly 96; Janie 94; Ted 92; George 90

Printed in Great Britain
by Amazon